THE CUSTOMER ISN'T ALWAYS RIGHT

THE CUSTOMER ISN'T ALWAYS RIGHT

KATHIE RODKEY

authorHOUSE®

AuthorHouse™
1663 Liberty Drive
Bloomington, IN 47403
www.authorhouse.com
Phone: 1-800-839-8640

Published by AuthorHouse   10/08/2012

ISBN: 978-1-4772-6854-4 (sc)
ISBN: 978-1-4772-6853-7 (e)

Library of Congress Control Number: 2012917138

DEDICATED TO EVERYONE
WHO HAS EVER WORKED IN RETAIL

CONTENTS

DOES ANY OF THE FOLLOWING SEEM FAMILIAR TO YOU?

Most people care about what might happen to the human race, unless they work in retail . . . . and then they don't give a crap.

Some stores are actually referring to their customers as guests, which is very appropriate. Most house guests begin to stink after three days, but when guests are shopping they stink after less than an hour.

Are you a person who honestly believes that when you return $50 worth of merchandise for which you received a $10 gift coupon that you still deserve to keep the coupon?

Do you leave a pile of clothes on the floor and sneak out of the fitting room when there are no employees looking?

Are you able to return a pocketbook you have used for a year complete with ink stains, appointment cards, old raisins and gum stuck to the inside and with a straight face demand your money back because the strap is somewhat frayed?

Do you throw a temper tantrum when you have to walk an extra couple of feet to receive a discount card for free merchandise?

Do you return clothing with no tags attached, with wine and cake stains on them stinking of cigarette smoke, perfume or body odor and swear they were never worn?

Then this book was written just for you.

On any given day, the retail environment is ripe with material for a television sitcom, part comedy and drama.

MS. DON'T MESS WITH ME represents the aggressive customers who slap, spit on or in other ways physically assault employees. During an early holiday opening, one so-called "lady" hit an employee with her pocketbook while he was trying to unlock the store, thinking he was cutting in line to take advantage of first come, first served specials.

MR. NOT MY ZIP CODE represents the many paranoid customers who go ballistic when asked to divulge their zip codes to the cashiers for a survey by corporate to determine in what areas they needed additional stores. He complained he didn't want to get any junk mail. The cashier tried not to laugh as she informed him that without the rest of his address it was not possible to send him anything. After all the drama and without blinking an eye, he paid for his purchase with a check which had all of his personal information on it. Of course, the paranoia is contagious and so the next customer in line also refused to give a zip code to the cashier.

Every day is like a three ring circus in retail. The manager is the ringmaster trying to cope with merchandise being stolen, ripped apart and left on the floor, employees calling off work or showing up late and inappropriately dressed and then taking long breaks and lunches, and customers either bringing food into the store or stealing it from the shelves and ruining merchandise with it. Then, just like under the big top, when the circus is over the cleanup begins . . . especially if the **URINATOR** or **KAKA PERSON** has been in the store.

THONG LADY personifies the many antics of senior shoppers. She leaves her shopping cart outside the restroom and a store employee mistakes it for a return cart. She throws a pair of thong underwear in it that she found shoved in a display toaster (that's a story for another time). Later, when **THONG LADY** placed her merchandise on the counter, the cashier who dumped the underwear in her cart was on the register and deliberately held up the thong, asking her if she wanted it. She glanced at the skimpy red underwear for just a second and responded with great enthusiasm that she absolutely did.

This gives new meaning to the term personal shopper! Just imagine how much additional revenue the store could take in if employees added items to all of the shopping carts.

Most cashiers earn minimum wage and work harder than people making three times that amount. Aside from standing on their feet for seven hours a day they must keep their registers straight, customers happy and the managers' content.

They also must deal with the following customer conspiracy. It's either feast or famine on the register lines.

Cashiers deserve more than what they make just for listening to Christmas music non-stop from Thanksgiving . . . no make that Halloween . . . to Christmas Eve.

To add insult to injury, cashiers who make next to nothing yet process thousands of dollars in sales a day are terminated for being over or under in the register drawer a couple of times within a short timetable. People with Ph.D.'s in finance would be hard pressed to last one day as a cashier on a slow day, let alone on a busy weekend or during the holiday season.

Retail employees are definitely not given the respect they deserve, nor do they feel as good about themselves and their profession as they should. Even those who start out with the most upbeat, good natured, keep smiling attitude lose it after only a few months on the job. For example, new employees will enthusiastically cut coupons out of the paper and present them to customers at the register for additional money off their purchase, but very soon they are tearing them up or hiding them. The longer they are on the register, the more beat up and cynical they become due to mistreatment by customers, managers, fellow associates and corporate. It is not a good feeling to realize that every customer has to be perceived as a possible scammer but still needs to be treated with kid gloves according to the mandates of corporate.

People who are sick in bed are in a better mood than most retail employees on any given day.

When **KAKA PERSON** is in the store, it is always a bad day. An associate enters the fitting room to find that this customer has defecated in one of the stalls and has used a piece of merchandise to wipe herself. There is no full time cleaning crew in the store, so either a really loyal associate with a strong stomach or the manager on duty must clean up the mess. It means getting the store item in a bag and identifying it as contaminated material needing to be damaged out.

Accidents courtesy of the **URINATORS** are more frequent, but no less disgusting, whether the yellow liquid comes from an adult or a child.

It is beyond coincidence that allowing people to eat or drink in stores also makes them more popular as pit stops for busloads of incontinent people who can't make it from point A to point B. Or a convenient drop off point for a 90-year old person who can barely walk and has already started taking a dump in his pants.

Other intimate finds are used sanitary napkins, dirty diapers and condoms which are left behind in the fitting rooms and other interesting places throughout the store, like the lingerie department or inside shoe boxes. Many times sanitary napkins seem to drop from the ceiling, leaving us wondering how they managed to escape the humans wearing them In addition there are the incontinent folks who leave a trail from one end of the store to the other, right up to the cash register and out the door. Instead of following the yellow brick road, retail employees follow the brown stained tile.

One of the cashiers started gagging immediately when she came upon a pile of poop and ran to the bathroom to throw up. Interestingly, she had just resigned from retail to start work in a nursing home of all things. Good luck with that.

Another associate who volunteered to clean up a mess asked for permission to take a break and smoke a cigarette to get the foul smell out of his nose. He is now proudly known as the **SHITMEISTER** and is looking for an increase in pay.

There are employees who don't even notice that someone is crapping on the floor. The unwritten rule is that the employee who sees it first cleans it up. Wait a second . . . maybe these workers aren't so clueless after all.

CASHIER PROSTITUTES . . . OOPS, I MEAN CASHIER PRODUCTIVITY

Most of the cashiers can't function until they look at the daily schedule to find out when their lunch and breaks are and who the manager on duty is. This is the person who will be doing all the yelling. Each manager has a different personality and approach to the job, so either it will be a good day or a bad day.

Before they open their registers, the cashiers are supposed to familiarize themselves with the items on sale, coupons being offered and other promotions.

A cashier starts out with a certain amount of money in the cash drawer at the beginning of each shift and this amount needs to be verified by them when they open their drawer for the day.

There are never enough people to staff the store, so employees who do show up for work are constantly taking on more duties. During slow periods, cashiers are expected to help unpack and put prices on merchandise, stock the end caps, do returns, clean up the aisles, fold tables and perform other duties as assigned. They are also expected to stay to recover the store after it closes.

In the last few years cashiers have become **CASHIER PROSTITUTES** . . . . selling everything but themselves at the register. At the same time, many corporations have instituted a production rating system assessing the cashier's scanning time and dollar activity. Someone sitting in an office, who most likely has never worked retail, actually believes that cashiers have some sort of control over how quickly a transaction can be completed.

These layers of administrative fat obviously don't know anything about the customer who doesn't begin to decide what they are buying until they get to the register . . . . this phenomenon is called *shopping at the register*. They ask the cashier, a friend or other people in line for advice on each piece of merchandise. Meanwhile, the scanning rating is ticking away as the cashier waits to ring up each piece of merchandise precious minutes apart from each other.

The upper level desk jocks at corporate who make the rules haven't taken into account the customer who makes loud rude remarks about how long other people's transactions are taking, while glaring at the cashier. Ironically, when it is their turn, this customer doesn't begin looking for their checkbook until the order is rung up, often times leaving the register to retrieve it while the other customers on line begin to howl.

When the customer returns to the scene, they start looking for a pen, ignoring the cashier's efforts to provide them with one. They then give the cashier a hard time when she asks for a phone number which is required on all checks. They then complain bitterly about the time it is taking for the check to be processed through the register. If it is a recycled check, it often times doesn't go through the printer requiring it to be handled manually.

The frantic cashier is now praying the check will be approved. If not, they must call it in, which is a fate worse than death.

If the check is declined, the cashier is then dealing with an irate customer who is obsessing about why the check was not approved. Some customers insist on calling the customer service number provided to argue about why their check was rejected before they will leave the register. Eventually, after an agonizing transaction, the order is put on suspense as the customer leaves the store to "find an ATM machine" or another form of payment. In most cases, they are usually never heard from again.

All the while, the cashier, not the customer whose check was declined, is the brunt of disgusted comments from the other customers in line. No matter what, the customers always stick together and perceive everything to be the cashier's fault.

Then there are the cash paying customers. Only after the total is rung up, do they begin looking for their money as if by some miracle what they purchased was going to be free of charge.

The cashier's productivity rating slips away minute by minute as the customer checks their pockets, purse or wallet for bills and coins. If there are two of them together, they banter back and forth about who has what in the way of change and bills. Some check each of their coins to make sure they are not giving away some precious antique or collectible. Some give up after two minutes realizing that they are not going to come up with sixty-two cents and then begin the process of finding more bills. Always, they make the same lame comments . . . . *I hate change, I want to lighten my load, I thought for sure I had enough . . . .*

And, of course, there are the customers who don't decide how to pay for their purchases until the items are rung up. All cashiers have experienced two, three, four and even five-tiered purchases. Keep in mind, the cashier is dealing with this while listening to the customer moan and groan about the time it is taking to complete the transaction, in addition to the insults from the other customers in line. Eventually, most cashiers find it best not to look up from the cash register at all.

MR. RUSH NO MORE is an example of the *idiotsyncrasies* (no . . . this is not a spelling error) of the customers at the cash register. This woman slams down her purchase and tells the cashier she is in a hurry, but suddenly decides that she forgot something and runs off. Her order is suspended while the cashier waits on another customer. She is furious when she comes back to the register ten minutes later and the cashier is waiting on someone else. She grabs her purchases from the counter and takes them to the next register, giving the new cashier the same story about being in a hurry. When she is finished, she leaves the register and walks over to a game at the exit door and proceeds to spend five minutes playing it . . . . so much for being in a hurry!

The cash drawer is in good shape until a customer comes along with a candy bar and pays for it with a $100 bill requiring the cashier to call for change. The customer immediately begins to make nasty comments about the time it is taking to get their $98.99 back. Presenting large bills for a small purchase is also part of a scam but more about that later.

MS. NO TORN MONEY FOR ME also qualifies as an idiot. She purchases gum and gives the cashier a fifty dollar bill. The cashier empties out the entire drawer of bills for change, but the customer decides she doesn't want one of the bills because it is slightly torn at the corner. The cashier patiently explains that she has no more bills to give her. The customer continues to complain and the weary cashier takes the defective bill and gives the customer a roll of dimes to replace the $5 bill that was torn. A bit vindictive you might say . . . . not at all.

Many customers need help processing their credit/debit cards through the machine and the cashier must be aggressive in helping them as their productivity is ticking away. If a call for approval code comes up, the cashier is required to call the credit card company in question. This is a timely process, most often resulting in the customer having to decide on another form of payment. Some credit cards look like they have been eaten by an animal. If the credit card is damaged, the cashier must hand key it in and then swipe a manual copy to prove it was in the store. Of course, the customer becomes very hyper about the swiping of their defective card and signing multiple statements.

Other reasons for delays in processing orders are customers who use gift cards, gift certificates and coupons to pay for their purchases; scanner malfunctions which require the cashier to hand key the product identification numbers until the computer can be shut down; merchandise that arrives at the register without a price tag requiring a call to the department for a price check; and items that have been mis-mated . . . the tops separated from the bottoms. The floor associate is called to reunite the correct sizes, while the customer complains vehemently that this is the way they found the item and this is the way they want it. In the majority of cases, the customer is long gone by the time the merchandise is mated by the employee.

Speaking of mis-mates, this is a hint to designers who don't put their name on all of their two and three piece garments. It is almost impossible to mate your products when they get separated from each other which results in lost sales for you. Put your designer name on all of your garments.

The eggheads at corporate don't realize how unfair the productivity rating can be. For example, some cashiers get lucky when they get a few big ticket items in their line resulting in a high scanning rating, while the unlucky cashier gets a cartful of small inexpensive items that take much longer to ring, giving them a low productivity score.

All shoes must be checked to make sure they are the same size and that the box contains a left and right shoe. If there is a security tag on the shoe, it must be removed. As luck would have it, the more people there are in the queue the more difficult it is to remove the tag.

MS. TWO LEFT FEET is a star in the foot fetish sitcom. She wants to buy a pair of shoes that are two left feet. She explains to the cashier that she has walked all over the store in them and they are the most comfortable shoes she has ever had on. The cashier calls the shoe manager who explains that he can't sell them unless he absolutely can't find the mates. At the customer's request, he walks away to search for the missing right shoes. The other customers in line glare at the cashier and it seems to take forever for the manager to return and announce that he can't find the right-footed shoes. More minutes pass while he decides on whether she can buy the two left shoes.

No doubt, at some point those two right shoes will show up in some nook, crevice or cranny in the store . . . . or possibly at the register in the hands of **MS TWO RIGHT FEET**.

On numerous occasions customers have been observed intently smelling the shoes and seemingly enjoying themselves. Employees quickly walk in the opposite direction away from these *smellers* . . . uh, customers.

During a visit from one of the secret shoppers, a shoe associate was asked what the difference was between man-made and leather shoes. He quickly replied that in his experience after wearing man-made shoes for a few days, a person's feet begin to stink. The store received a write-up and no points for that response. The associates laughed for days, but management was not amused.

When a customer questions the price on an item, it causes a delay. If the merchandise is defective, the customer will ask for a reduction in the price. The cashier needs to call the manager to see if an additional discount can be given. Many times, merchandise that is damaged can be returned to the manufacturer for full price, so there is a limit on the amount of money the store can give a customer.

MS. DAMAGED IT MYSELF is the customer who used a ball point pen to make dents in the side of a decorative mirror to get an additional discount. When approached by an employee, she said she was testing it to make sure it would hold up when she got it home. She was obviously planning on using it as a dartboard.

So, if a cashier seems frazzled, it may be due to the following: unhappy customers, computer malfunctions, scanning errors, production rating, credit card problems, voids, coupons, gift cards, promotions, switched tickets, scams, traveler's checks, schedules, emergency codes, and shortages.

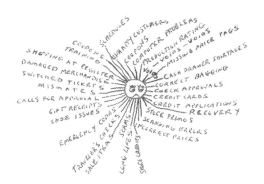

Lately, customers are complaining about all of the questions that are being asked at the register. In just a few short years, the following items have been added to the cashier responsibilities, resulting in the term *cashier prostitutes*.

1. SELL THOSE CREDIT CARDS.

Cashiers are required to solicit customers to open store credit card accounts at the register. This is a process which can be fraught with stress especially when the store is busy. The customer must fill out an application and present a major credit card and a form of I.D., usually their license. The cashier then must scan the credit card and put information into a computerized form; the application is either approved or declined. The cashier then writes down the credit card number and driver's license number on the application along with the new credit card number printed on the customer's temporary credit card. If the cashier is lucky, and the customer is approved on the first try, the customer's order is then processed. If they are declined, they sometimes present another credit card and the process starts all over again.

MS. YOU'RE CUT OFF is the customer who presents three different credit cards to the cashier, all of which result in her being declined for the store credit card. After each rejection, she insists the cashier is doing something wrong, announcing that her husband's job allows them to afford anything. Eventually, she decides to pay for the purchase with her existing credit cards, all of which are declined. She has a child with her who appears to be about 10 years old, who keeps telling her mother "you needs to talk to daddy". The little girl kept repeating it as the mother walked away in a huff, minus any purchases, ignoring the child and mumbling about the ineptness of the cashier.

MS. I SHOULD APPLY, I SHOULDN'T APPLY, I SHOULD APPLY . . . . represents the customers who can't make a decision. In some cases, the purchase is rung up with another form of payment and then the customer decides to apply for a credit card requiring the transaction to be voided by a manager, much to the chagrin of the people waiting in line. In other cases, the customer decides after everything is processed and a hefty discount given for applying for a credit card, to opt out of the commitment resulting in manager involvement and register delays.

The cashier is also responsible for issuing a temporary credit card if the customer has forgotten to bring their credit card. This requires the guest to provide their identification and put their social security number in the pin pad. In many cases, the customer complains loudly about the process being an invasion of privacy, rather than quietly inserting the number in a pin pad, which no one else can see them doing. The solution is simple . . . . bring your credit card the next time you shop.

Last, but not least, are the customers who try to open up a store credit card with library, telephone and other department store cards, some which have expired years ago.

2. SOLICIT THOSE E-MAILS AND GUEST LOYALTY CARDS

These mechanisms allow corporate to give customers coupons and other incentives to shop the store, requiring the cashiers to ask each guest if they would like to sign up and why it is in their best interest to do so. Then they need to process their personal information, focusing on getting e-mail addresses and phone numbers. Some customers opt out halfway through, deciding that the process requires too much personal information.

3. SELL SURVEY PROGRAMS, SUSCRIPTIONS OR CHARITY CONTRIBUTIONS.

Special promotions require the cashiers to ask the guests to contribute or sign up. Magazine subscriptions and other incentives are offered to the customers by the cashiers if they use their credit card. Money for charities is sometimes collected at the register and many stores ask employees to participate in charity events during their non-working time. Cashiers are required to talk to customers before they leave the register about completing store surveys.

4. MERCHANDISE WARRANTIES are another item that has been added to the cashier duties. They must ask each customer purchasing qualifying merchandise if they want the plan and then process the required information into the register.

The customers are usually so annoyed by all of the requests that they end up being rude to the cashier as if it was their fault and not a critical part of their job.

The company employs secret shoppers who show up unannounced to make sure cashiers are asking the right questions. If the company doesn't use secret shoppers, the managers are always surfing the registers listening to the cashiers.

I'LL HELP THE NEXT SCAMMER...
I MEAN CUSTOMER

Aside from being burdened with too many duties at the register which makes for longer lines and more irate customers, the cashiers must also worry about customer scams and other questionable transactions.

MR. HURRY UP showed up at the register on a busy Saturday, talking on his cell phone. During the transaction, he told the cashier his wife had been in a car accident and he needed to leave immediately. He gave the cashier what she thought was five twenty dollar bills to pay for his order and insisted that she hurry so he could get to the hospital. Later, the cashier realized that in the middle of the four twenty dollar bills was one five dollar bill. The register came up short and the cashier was written up.

MS. HOLIDAY CHEER is the scammer who works with a fellow crook usually during the holiday rush. One of them presents the cashier with a gift certificate, which is processed as a cash transaction. In this scam, the customer deliberately does not sign the back of the gift certificate, knowing the cashier will return it in order to get a signature. Meanwhile, the customer's accomplice is piling her stuff on top of the counter to further confuse the cashier. Just as the customer hoped for, the cashier forgets to ask for the gift certificate back. This results in a significant cash shortage in the register drawer and a write-up for the cashier.

The **QUICK CHANGE ARTIST** is the customer who tries to confuse the cashier by changing the monetary form of payment several times during the transaction, until the cashier is so confused they end up giving the customer back more money than they should have. This scammer always targets new cashiers.

The **ROLF OF DIMES** scammer shows up when the store is extremely busy and gives a new cashier a roll of coins to pay for the purchase. The cashier accepts it and does not open it up. The roll has a dime at either end, but in the middle are pennies.

The **SWITCHED TICKET** scammer takes high priced tickets off merchandise and replaces them with lower priced tickets. These customers have their own equipment to reattach the tickets professionally. These scammers also place two items on the same hanger, hoping the cashier will think they are together and get them both for the price of one. They also stack household items like mixing bowls inside of each other to get three for the price of one. They put expensive curtains in promotional curtain bags and stuff suitcases and pocketbooks with merchandise, hoping that the cashier doesn't open them up.

MR. BUY THE BAG, NOT THE GIFT is the customer who buys a huge birthday gift bag and places merchandise neatly in the fold of the bag, hoping it will not be noticed by the cashier. It is even sadder when parents do this and other types of scams in front of their children.

CHECK FOR LESS is another very common and surprisingly successful scam. The customer writes a check for much less than the purchase and hopes the busy cashier doesn't notice. These savvy people watch for new cashiers who are already harried.

Corporate will not challenge these customers to avoid insulting them, but the cashier is written up for a register shortage.

As technology gets more sophisticated, so does the shoplifting techniques. The cashier is responsible for assuring they don't take counterfeit money or coupons. Unfortunately, most of the blue light indicators developed to quickly assess the validity of a bill don't work and the pen is no longer a reliable way of catching bogus money. Better have good eyes to hold the money up to the light and examine it closely, while the customer glares. Most cashiers don't really know what the heck they are looking for anyway.

Due to staff shortages, cashiers who have only been on the register a day or two themselves are training new cashiers . . . talk about the blind leading the blind.

Eventually, no matter what productivity rating program is in place, as the cashiers become more experienced they become less rushed, looking carefully at every bill and check received and religiously counting incoming cash and change to the customer. In the end, they realize the repercussions to them are much greater for shortages at the register as opposed to low productivity.

THE GOOD, THE BAD,
AND THE UGLY

There are some very endearing customers as evidenced by the following:

MR. INTERVIEW hurries into the store in a jogging outfit, goes to the men's department and picks out a suit, tie and shirt. He runs to the register and pays for his purchases, then asks if he can use the dressing room to change because he is late for a job interview. As he is running out of the store, a cashier yells at him to stop so she can cut off the tags hanging from his new clothes.

MS. FIRST NEW SUIT comes to the register with a suit for her husband, remarking that she hopes it will fit him as it is much more expensive than she thought it would be. She adds that it is the first suit he has ever worn. The cashier informs her that the suit can be returned if it doesn't fit, but nothing could have prepared her for the women's reply. She said that she definitely wouldn't be returning the suit because her husband was being buried in it. The cashier had just lost her husband and started crying.

MR. SPLIT PERSONALITY comes into the store dressed in a suit jacket, button-down shirt and tie, with shorts, white knee-high socks and sneakers. He obviously couldn't decide whether he wants to be at work or on vacation.

MR. THONG MAN who thinks he is all that comes into the store wearing white see-through shorts with red thong underwear clearly visible underneath them. To make matters worse, he has a pot belly and legs full of varicose veins and walks like he just had a hemorrhoid operation. On the other hand, it could have been because of the thong up his butt.

MS. HAIRY BLOUSE rushes into the store and picks out a 90% clearance blouse to put on before she gets her hair cut and dyed, telling the cashier she doesn't want to ruin the expensive blouse she has on. Interestingly, the blouse she is buying for $1.50 is far nicer than the one she is wearing.

MR. ALMOST MADE IT, an older gentleman, is literally holding up his pants while he finds a belt. He makes it to the register, but becomes so involved in paying for his purchase he takes his hands off of his pants and they immediately fall down.

MR. FORGOT MY BELT is the customer who comes in to the store frantically looking for a belt to replace the one he forgot to put on that morning. His pants are held up with safety pins. Other customers use a variety of things from duct tape to string to paper clips.

MR. UNDERWEAR is the generous customer who buys a suitcase and fifty pairs of packaged underwear to send to his country; coincidentally, the same country where the underwear is made. He tells the cashier the people who work in the factory can't afford to buy the clothing.

MR. DROPPED HIS PANTS is in such a hurry he doesn't give the cashier time to tie a knot at the end of the plastic bag covering his suit. As he leaves the register, the cashier notices his pants have fallen off the suit hanger onto the floor. She runs after the customer screaming at the top of her lungs, "Sir, you dropped your pants". It was amusing seeing everyone's head turn to get a glimpse of a half-naked man.

MS. WONDERBALLS places a pair of men's underwear and two boxes of Wonder Balls (chocolate candy) on the register. The cashier starts laughing hysterically as she processes the purchase. The customer also starts laughing when she realizes what she has done. Soon, everyone in the vicinity is snickering.

MS. CROSS LADY visits the store on religious holidays carrying a big wooden cross and a bible and preaching to anyone who will listen. This is against store policy, but she is harmless and very endearing so no one bothers her.

MS. WREATH comes in on special occasions to buy a flower arrangement for her daughter's gravesite, and has the cashiers in tears talking about the circumstances of her child's untimely death. On each of her visits, she asks if we sell twine so she can attach the wreath to the gravestone. The house wares associate retrieves the string she keeps in the receiving room just for this purpose and gives it to Ms. Wreath free of charge.

MR. PROCASTINATOR rushes up to the register on Mother's Day with a blouse in his hand, complaining he had to get it to his mom before the end of the day. He was elated when the cashier informed him that Mother's Day was a week away, and he immediately canceled the order. The cashier was sure he would be back in line the following Sunday, as frantic as ever.

MS. CODE EVE panics as the store is closing because she can't find her daughter. The manager calls a Code Adam and several of the associates immediately began looking for the girl in all of the usual places: toy department, bathrooms, fitting room, and under the garment racks. Suddenly, the mother points to her child and the manager watches in astonishment as a six-foot tall girl, about 19-years old walks into the store from the mall. The missing child is bigger than her mother and older than a couple of the associates who were looking for her.

MS. NEVER ENDING TRUNK pulls up to the front of the store in a tiny clown car. The box she wants loaded in her car is practically as long as her car. Everyone gathers at the door to see how the associate assisting her is going to perform a miracle and clap in amazement as the box disappears into the car. In this case, both the miniscule back and passenger seats collapsed down making it possible for the box to fit into the car. Most of the time, customers have to put their purchases on hold until they can find an appropriate vehicle to transport them home.

MR. GREEN BRA takes a toaster out of his cart and places it on the counter. He reaches into the cart for the next item and has a look of bewilderment on his face when he sees a bright green bra in his hand. His face turns beet red as he finally realizes the cart is not his.

MS. TROLLEY runs up to the cashier complaining loudly someone stole her "trolley" (shopping cart). Ms. Trolley immediately begins chastising Mr. Green Bra when she recognizes her stuff in his cart. Poor Mr. Green Bra never found his cart; it just wasn't his day.

There are many customers who give other customers money when they are short, who pick up merchandise when they drop it, who don't shoplift, who don't eat and drink in the store, who say thank you and please, who smile and wait patiently in line knowing it is part of the process. People working in retail appreciate each and every one of them.

Unfortunately, there are more of the following types of customers:

MR. AND MRS. EAT, DRINK AND BE SLOPPY come into the store drinking coffee and open up a bag of gourmet cookies from the food aisle They leave their half-filled coffee cups and half-eaten cookies among the merchandise for the employees, AKA . . . waiters and waitresses, to dispose of. Every day, hot dogs, hamburgers, sub sandwiches, pretzels, cookies, donuts and other food items brought into the store are found half-eaten in every department. Thousands of dollars of merchandise is damaged-out in stores every year from food and drink.

MR. (OR MS.) HOW GROSS CAN WE GET is the customer who places a half-eaten ice cream cone on a package of white socks. By the time the floor associate sees it, the chocolate ice cream is totally melted into the socks and the cone is hard as a rock, giving the item the appearance of a used sanitary napkin someone has defecated into. The associates had to be restrained from sending it to corporate as an example of why people shouldn't be allowed to eat or drink in the store.

Gum is found attached to just about everything: shelves, clothing, food, furniture, toys, towels, hats and shoes.

Opened candy ends up everywhere . . . . sticky, unfinished lollipops attached to whatever they land on and smashed, melted, half eaten chocolate candy hidden behind toys and in underwear and bras.

Customers actually do not believe they are shoplifting when they eat merchandise they have not paid for.

Owners of the company don't seem concerned about the damage to the merchandise from spilled food or the fact that the store is considered less upscale by the same customers who trash it with their food.

A question to retailers who allow food and drink to be consumed in stores. *WHAT ARE YOU THINKING?* **It's a no-win situation.**

And now for the really, really ugly customers:

MS BOOGER MOM is the customer who picks her child's nose and wipes the boogers on a men's dress shirt, which fortunately is wrapped in plastic. The employee witnessing the incident is so outraged she quickly grabs a piece of tissue paper from another shirt and tries to hand it to the customer, who refused to take it. The livid associate, in an exaggerated move, then wipes the boogers off the shirt and throws the soiled paper into the customer's basket.

MS. NO WRINKLED MONEY is the customer who goes nuts when she sees a cashier crumpling up some new dollar bills she was giving out as change. She demands the cashier "not wrinkle her bills". Ironically, the customer forgot an item and soon was back in line, using the change she had just gotten to pay for her purchase. The cashier returned two dollars to *Ms. No Wrinkled Money* commenting that she just gave her too much money because the new bills stuck together. Not surprisingly, the customer just glared at the cashier, too stubborn and ignorant to even say thank you.

MOM AND POPS FREE BABYSITTING SERVICE involves the people who come into the store and immediately drop their kids off in the toy department, usually with lollipops in their mouths or ice cream cones in their hands. The parents then disappear into another area of the store or shopping center leaving the children by themselves. These young people run wild through the store knocking merchandise off shelves, playing on railings, throwing pillows around, shoplifting and spilling food all over the merchandise and floor.

There is a Code Adam for lost children, but there should be a Code Jerk for lost adults. In one instance, a four year old boy was separated from his parents for about ten minutes. When his father finally showed up, he picked the child up by his ear, twisting it so hard that he started to cry. The employees who were mothers had to be restrained from hurting this Code Jerk and instead settled for hurling some unprintable words at him.

All employees are amazed at how few kidnappings occur in retail considering the number of young children that are left unsupervised in the store. Many a Code Adam is announced but usually after several minutes of searching, most of the children are found squirreled up in a garment rack.

MR. AND MRS. IT'S ALL ABOUT ME are the parents who bring their children into the store to shop when they are hungry and exhausted and then slap them silly when they don't stop crying. Retail associates witness children getting hit with everything from hangers to shoe boxes, but there is great reluctance to interfere as it could mean the loss of their job for antagonizing a customer.

MS. MULTI-TASKER feeds her child as she shops. The baby spits out every mouthful of food all over the cart and merchandise and onto the floor. Her mother ignores the mess and makes no attempt to clean it up.

THE BARTERERS are customers who think they are still in a country where dickering for goods is the acceptable way to do business and spend lots of time at the register begging the cashiers and managers to reduce prices or give them a free item.

MS. I'M NEVER SATISFIED are the customers who are eligible for $30 worth of free merchandise during their next visit to the store, but complain bitterly about having to walk to another part of the store to collect their coupon. These are the same people who go ballistic if they have to pay tax on the items they are getting free.

MS. IT'S NEVER ENOUGH are the customers who are always unhappy with the price of an item.

To the retailers who consistently don't make the day in sales because of multiple discounts given to customers, causing registers to freeze or crash, isn't it easier and more cost-efficient to reduce the price of the merchandise? Not to mention saving a few trees by reducing paperwork.

There are no words to describe the actions of retailers giving "surprise discounts" to customers when they are at the register with their purchases and mentally prepared to pay a certain amount for them.

Coupons should be used strictly to get customers into the store; once they are there, it makes no sense to surprise them with more discounts.

Of course, there are shoppers who definitely deserve to be signaled out for recognition:

To the customer who complained bitterly that he was being robbed when his Frito Lay order rang up $4.98, because the advertisement said 3 for $5. It took a long time to convince him that he actually was paying two cents less than the advertisement for this purchase.

To the customers who congregate at the entrance to the register socializing, while customers try to maneuver around them to get in line to pay for their purchases. They then have the audacity to harass the cashier when she asks them kindly to step aside.

To the customers who leave their credit card and merchandise at the register while they wander off looking for a forgotten item.

To the customers who allow their children to stand in the shopping carts, play with fixtures and run around the store as if it were a playground.

To the customers who leave pocketbooks and merchandise in their carts and proceed to shop three aisles away from them.

To the customers who call to say they lost money in the store and demand to be notified when it is found.

SERVICING THE CUSTOMERS

If you are a person who truly likes to be abused, then being a Customer Service Representative (CSR) is your dream job.

Recently, a customer informed everyone within hearing distance that people were stabbed by someone in the customer service area of another store. There is no doubt this scenario could play out very easily in the return environment. It is one thing to be a cashier waiting on customers buying items, but it is another thing to deal with them when they are bringing them back.

For example, a customer with a huge smile on her face attempts to return three worn and dirty items that do not belong to the store. Her smile quickly turns to a frown when she is challenged by the CSR. She asks for a manager and after a very tense few minutes of heated discourse, the manager approves the return leaving the shopper emboldened and the customer service representative deflated and mistreated further by the customer.

The premise behind the store manager's action is retail-wide and relates to the overall attitude that the monetary loss from damaged items, even if they do not belong to the store, is not enough to warrant going into battle with the customer. They are also afraid they will be held accountable by corporate for antagonizing a customer, despite the fact this so-called customer is a shoplifter! Why corporate values customers who are thieves is a mystery.

Rules are made to be broken in customer service and different managers make different decisions in similar circumstances. The CSR's are **ALWAYS** the bad cops, never knowing which way a manager will react to a return.

Unfortunately, word gets out that the store is an easy mark and the retailer loses big money each year on customer scams.

CSR's make a little bit more per hour than cashiers. Their duties include opening and closing registers, getting change for the cashiers, answering calls involving problems at the registers, processing returns, assisting with the midday pickup of money at the registers, and helping floor associates with their departments.

The CSR's most important job is to keep the customers happy and this is a difficult task when they are returning items. The psychology behind buying items is much different than the psychology of returning items. The customer doing a return is already dissatisfied with something and ready for a fight. The glares from customers waiting in the customer service line are 100% more hostile than the glares from customers waiting in the cashier line.

The return policies, especially unlimited and 90-day periods, allow many cunning customers to buy a coat in winter, wear it all season and return it in the spring for a raincoat. Wear the raincoat all spring and return it in the summer for a shawl, wearing it all season and returning it in the fall for a light jacket. No way, you say! It's been done many, many times.

Despite a policy which requires items being returned to be in saleable condition, customers consistently get away with returning clothes that reek of cigarette smoke, body and food odors, are stained with makeup, deodorant, sweat and food, are covered with animal hair, and look as if they have been slept in.

A well-stocked service desk always includes a bottle of strong deodorizer to spray on returned clothing before they go back on the floor for an unsuspecting customer to buy.

The CSR's job is made harder these days because a lot of clothes are sold distressed and look like they have been worn for years. When they are returned, it is difficult to assess whether they are used or were sold with holes in them. Some of these items wouldn't be accepted by a charitable organization they are in such bad condition.

There are all kinds of scams associated with customer returns.

MR. FOUR ALL SEASONS walks into the store in September with a patio umbrella he bought in June and announces that it is broke. The umbrella has bird crap and grease stains on it. Because this man is within the 90-day return period and has his receipt, he receives a full refund on the umbrella which he obviously used all summer long. He immediately goes to the seasonal department where he picks up a rake for the fall which he obviously will return after 90 days for something for the winter.

MS. AND MR. A LITTLE BIT AT A TIME are the customers who buy items with a promotional coupon and then return them the next day for full store credit. They don't bring the receipt and say it was a gift so they won't lose the discount they received the day before.

For example, they purchase a $20.99 dress with a 20% off coupon and receive $4.19 off. They then return the item without the receipt and receive a store credit for the full $20.99. Each time they do this they have more money to spend on other items, and the store is losing big bucks over time.

Another example of this scam involves suit sales. The customer buys two suits for a certain price but the discount is taken off of only one suit. A month later, when the sale is forgotten, they bring back the full priced suit, again without a receipt, for a full store credit. They now have a suit back home which they paid half price or less for and have returned a suit for full price credit. Again, the store loses.

MR. AND MS. STEAL IT AND RETURN IT. These are customers who steal an item or items and immediately bring them to customer service for return.

On one occasion, the security guard followed a man to the customer service desk after observing him loading his cart with a vacuum cleaner and other big ticket items. The manager was called to the desk and talked to the customer briefly, mentioning that he was not observed bringing the return items into the store. The customer became irate and the manager quickly backed down, instructing the customer service rep to give him a store credit for the stolen items even though he didn't have a receipt.

Meanwhile, the security guard was hiding in the bra fixture, shaking her head at the CSR not to give the man anything for the merchandise. After the manager walked away, the customer service rep took a very big chance and told the customer that there were security cameras, pointing to the one above her head, and that they did not show him coming into the store with the merchandise and that if he accepted a store credit, he could be prosecuted. He slammed his hand down hard on the counter, shouted loudly about people not trusting him, abandoned his cart and walked away, yelling that he was going home to get his receipt. He never came back.

Unfortunately, most customers get away with this scam because the CSR, the manager, or the security agent will not take the chance of losing their jobs by challenging the thief.

FILL ER UP! These customers love stores that don't require them to check bags. They bring used or cheap dollar store items in their bags, pick out more expensive merchandise to bring into the fitting room, and then put the more expensive items into the bag and put the cheap items on the hangers. This scam works extremely well especially in fitting rooms with no attendants. Even if the room is attended, on most days the fitting room clerk does not have enough time to inspect with a fine tooth comb exactly what is on the hanger as they are counted. These shoplifters bring special tools to remove tags and replace them on other merchandise.

NASTY BRA: A disgusted customer brings a bra to the service desk which looks like it has been worn every day for four years, saying she found it on the bra rack. There are a couple of scenarios for how it got there: after a shoplifter treated herself to a new bra she put her old bra on the hanger and slipped it back on the rack to avoid security issues, or left the old bra in the fitting room where it was scooped up by a harried lingerie employee who placed it on a hanger while trying to do returns as quickly as possible.

This bra was so disgusting the young CSR scooped it up with a hangar so she wouldn't have to touch it as she carried it back to the damage area, like a white flag signaling her surrender.

The ironic thing about this scenario is that the customer said it was hanging with the same-sized bras. It must have been a coincidence because very rarely do our new bras get put back on the right rack, let alone a bra where the label is practically non-existent.

The lingerie department is completely trashed by the customer each day. To be fair, however, the kind of hangers that are used for panties and bras are useless, breaking easily and causing the merchandise to fall on the floor. Intimate apparel should be featured in baskets by size.

As an associate was picking up her hundredth pair of underpants one day, a customer adamantly questioned her about returning them to the rack after they had been on the floor. She quickly pointed out to the customer that if she damaged out all of the underwear that fell on the floor, there wouldn't be anything left in the department to sell.

Ironically, this is the same customer who wouldn't think anything of returning a pair of underwear she had used for six months, skid marks and all.

BUY ONE, STEAL ONE FREE: These customers purchase an item and exit the store. They then come back in with the receipt only, pick up an identical item and return it to customer service for a full refund. The identical item, which is in their car, is now free . . . . and stolen.

TWO, THREE OR FOUR FOR THE PRICE OF ONE: The customer stuffs two bras in a box priced for one bra, puts four pairs of socks in a box priced for two socks, puts four pairs of underwear in a box priced for one pair, puts two pillowcases in a bag made for one, and puts sheets in a comforter bag. On a busy day, it is difficult for a cashier to open and inspect every box and bag that comes to the register. Some of these customers then return the original item in the box for a refund, keeping the shoplifted items.

THE LUCKY SHOPLIFTER: An associate caught this customer in home fashions stuffing a bag with a sofa cover. The associate asked her if she had a receipt for the items she was putting in the bag. She became indignant screaming that she did indeed have a receipt and that she was returning items.

The associate offered to take her bags to the returns desk until she was ready to complete the transaction. When she finally did make it to customer service, the receipts she presented were old and did not match the items that were in the bags. Because there was no security that day, the associate could not prove that this shoplifter came into the store with empty bags and no merchandise. The guest received a substantial store credit on items that she had just stolen from the store. It is likely that the customer called the store and asked for security prior to coming in to make sure they were not on duty (more about that in the security section).

MR. AND MRS. MISMATE: She's pear shaped and he's built like a light bulb. They buy two suits for him and two suits for her but ask for four separate receipts. When they get home, he takes the jacket from one of the suits and the pants from the other to make his own custom combination. She does the same with her two suits. The next day, they bring back the two suits that are now mis-mated swearing that was the way they purchased them. Because they have separate receipts, the CSR does not know they purchased two other suits. They end up with suits at home that fit them perfectly and the store ends up with mis-mated suits that eventually get damaged out or put on sale at a reduced price for another light bulb or pear to buy.

I DIDN'T GET MY MERCHANDISE: A month after purchase, a customer comes in and complains they didn't get an item on the receipt. Incredulous, the CSR tells her that nothing can be done and that she should have brought this to the attention of management immediately. The customer puts up a stink and a retail-weary manager approves a duplicate item for the customer. Feeling empowered, the customer goes one step further proclaiming it was actually two items she didn't get. Again, the manager approves a second item. By the way, most managers approve or disapprove these transactions over the store phone so they don't have to come to the customer service desk and deal with the CSR or the customer face-to-face.

SHOE TALES: Customers return shoes that are well-worn but have a receipt dated within the 90-day return period. These people actually have the colossal nerve to complain that they are returning them because they didn't fit right.

Corporate executives came up with another of their lame schemes giving customers a coupon worth 20% off a new pair of shoes if they brought in an old pair of shoes. The associates were completely baffled . . . . why would customers take advantage of a promotion like that when they are allowed to return their old shoes for a full price refund? Not surprisingly, this promotion was a complete bust.

THE SHOE SWITCHER approaches the register wearing her new shoes and hands the cashier a price tag. Because the tag was no longer attached to the shoe, the cashier calls the shoe manager to verify the price. The shoes on her feet were $39.99, not $19.00 with 75% off as the tag the customer presented to the cashier indicated.

The customer was completely irate that the cashier would question her integrity by checking the price. She took the shoes off her feet, slammed them down on the counter and walked out barefoot, holding her well-worn old shoes.

WHEN ALL ELSE FAILS, BLEACH IT. This customer took the security tag off his sneakers and then tried to get rid of the ink stains with bleach. When he returned them, the CSR could smell the bleach as soon as he walked in the door. Interestingly enough, in this case the customer did not steal the shoes and would have had no problem bringing them back to get the security tag taken off.

PARTY AND THEN RETURN customers bring back worn formal dresses, tuxedos and suits stained with deodorant, makeup and food, reeking with odors, and ripped.

After suffering tremendous monetary losses because of this scam, some smart retail executives changed their policy so that social suits and separates cannot be returned without the tags intact. They actually started printing the policy on the receipts for those customers who just don't get it. Still, many retailers allow return of social items without tags and with no time limit.

Have you ever been to an event where the tag on a dress or suit frees itself from its hiding place without the person wearing the item knowing? You can bet they will be returning the outfit to the store the next day.

CAT'S COMFORTER: This customer asked the home accessories associate to help her pick out a comforter for her son's bed. She said it had to be dark because the cat slept with her son and threw up all the time.

Two weeks later, she brought the comforter back saying that it didn't work out. Looking through the plastic, the associate could see the comforter was covered with cat hair and throw-up stains. Incredulously, management approved this outrageous return.

I SWEAR WE DIDN'T USE THAT are the customers who lie. One scammer returned an ice cream machine insisting it had not been used. She made the mistake of bringing her four-year old child with her who announced for all to hear that they did use the item, reminding her mother repeatedly how badly the chocolate ice cream tasted. Each time the mother denied it had been used, the child contradicted her even louder.

THE TEN-CENT ITEMS are the most amusing returns. The customer waits just a bit too long to return an item (usually years), without a receipt. The item has been marked down so low that it is considered a ten-cent item. There are customers who actually get a store credit for ten cents rather than keep the item or give it to charity.

Speaking of waiting years to return items, many customers receive full refunds on these returns if they have a receipt even though the items are only worth ten cents to the store.

THE ORANGE AFFAIR customer throws a dress on the counter and announces with disgust she is returning it because it turned everything in her washing machine orange. She continues complaining bitterly that she should be reimbursed for other clothes that were ruined. The CSR reads the instructions label on the dress and points out that this particular item should have been washed by hand in cold water. Even after the CSR agrees to return the dress, the customer continues to make a case for additional reimbursement. She didn't ask to speak to a manager but if she had she most likely would have received whatever she demanded from a supervisor afraid of a complaint to corporate.

MR. AND MS. I WANT MORE MONEY BACK THAN WHAT I PAID FOR IT are the customers who return items and complain bitterly about being cheated when the clearance or promotional prices are taken off the return amount. Often it takes many minutes of explanation and staring at the receipt before the customers understand they are being reimbursed exactly what they paid for the item.

MR. AND MS. STORE CREDIT are the customers who spend agonizing amounts of time questioning the balance on cards they were issued for store credit. The CSR ends up calling corporate to confirm the balance on the card and if it isn't the amount the customer thinks it should be, must listen to accusations of thievery and incompetence from them.

Another customer shoved a year old receipt in the CSR's face, complaining that she didn't get a merchandise credit with her return. When the CSR confirmed that a merchandise credit was issued on the return and spent, the customer accused the CSR of stealing the card. She continued to rant even after the associate informed her that she just started working for the store and couldn't possibly have "stolen" her card.

THE PROMOTIONAL ABUSERS buy merchandise and receive money-off coupons to use for future purchases. Later, they return the items they originally purchased and when the CSR asks for the promotional coupon they insist they never got it. They are not challenged and most likely have already used the coupon. This scam costs retail stores big bucks every day. In these tough times, many retailers are programming computers to automatically take the promotional amount off of the return items. Of course, the CSR's must then spend inordinate amounts of time explaining to irate customers why money is being taken off of their return items.

Store owners should insist that the coupon numbers be recorded on the receipts so they can easily be confiscated when merchandise is returned by the customer. Better yet, promotional coupons should be printed out along with the register receipt so they are a package deal when items are returned. Promotional programs should be properly monitored to prevent abuse as they account for millions of dollars of loss by retail stores every year.

MR. AND MS. TEMPORARY CREDIT CARD arrive at the CSR desk saying they forgot their credit card and are issued a temporary one. They know when they get to the register with the temporary paper card the cashier will automatically assume they just opened a new account and give them a significant percentage off their purchase.

Some retailers figured out what was going on and required the associates issuing the temporary credit cards to indicate that it was not a new account on the printout. Unfortunately, especially when the store is very busy, the CSR or cashier forgets this important part of the transaction and the scam continues. Other stores are yet to catch on.

So, for all those retailers who enable shoplifters and scammers with their loosey-goosey practices, here is some advice:

To the company that allows returns without receipts:
It's time for people to take responsibility for keeping track of their receipts. Customers frequently return items within 15 minutes of purchase announcing they have already lost their receipts.

To the company that doesn't hire door greeters to monitor a package check-in system:
When customers are allowed to shop the store with bags of merchandise it makes it easier for them to shoplift. A door greeter is worth their weight in gold.

To the company that doesn't monitor fitting rooms:
Millions of dollars in merchandise is stolen every year in fitting rooms because cameras are not allowed, and shoplifters know it. The fitting room attendant is one of the most important people in the store. With proper attention to the job, most of the shoplifting in this area can be prevented. The fitting rooms should never be left unattended from the time the store opens until it closes.

To the company allowing customers to bring merchandise bags into the bathrooms and fitting rooms:

Again, this practice would be eliminated with a package check-in system. Along with the massive amounts of merchandise tags left on the floor of the fitting rooms, the toilets in the bathrooms are often clogged with price tags from stolen merchandise.

To the company that doesn't monitor the men's fitting rooms:

Men shoplift also. They enter the fitting room with several packages of underwear and exit wearing several pairs of underwear. The empty bags are blatantly left in the fitting room.

On a side note, associates are thinking of putting a ROOM FOR RENT sign on a door in both the male and female fitting rooms for couples who use them. One pair left behind ten bathing suits and a used condom in one of the rooms. That was some pool party.

To the company conducting buy one, get one free sales (BOGO):

Instead of one item on the BOGO being listed as free and one item as full price, both items should show half off on the receipt. This prevents a customer from returning the full price item months later without an alert CSR catching the fact it was part of a BOGO.

To the company taking back shoes which have been worn for months, as well as other well-used merchandise:

Enabling these thieves to scam the store hurts your valued customers by increasing the prices they pay for merchandise to offset the loss. This practice is so prevalent and ridiculous a store took back a recliner which had been used for three years because the customers complained it wouldn't recline anymore. The chair smelled so gross it had to be taken out of the store immediately to the nearest dumpster by two employees wearing plastic gloves and masks.

To the company that gives money or merchandise to customers who come in days or months after making a purchase claiming that the cashier didn't give them an item:

If a customer does not make a case for a missing item within 24 hours of their purchase, they should not be given a replacement item.

To the company that doesn't put up signs informing customers that bras, panties and bathing suits cannot be returned without the tags in place claiming they don't want to "offend" the customers:

There is nothing more offensive to an employee than having to take back intimate items without tags but with skid marks and other stains on them.

To the company that doesn't stand by their policy not to take back social items without tags attached:

Customers return these items after wearing them to weddings or funerals, insisting that the tags were not on the item when they were purchased. Depending on the manager on duty, they usually get away with this form of shoplifting.

To the company that doesn't stand by ALL of the policies they incorporate:

Customers are not in kindergarten anymore. If they are mature, they should be able to abide by the store's policies knowing it is in their best interest to do so. If not, they are not worth having as customers.

To the company that doesn't defend their managers and associates against abusive customers.

Shame on you! While your hard-working employees get treated like dirt by customers who continuously get their way despite the fact they are incapable of treating anyone with respect, they return time and time again like a bad penny to continue their abuse, scams and shoplifting. They are not your valued customers.

Some managers need advice also:

-**Do not ignore employees who don't do their jobs.** Write them up and fire them instead of looking to your worker bees to pick up the slack. This is considered inequitable treatment and causes hostility among the employees, resulting in burnout and frequent turnovers.

-**Help your employees when they are busy.** Don't be adverse to performing cashier duties, folding items on a table or picking items off of the floor. The employees will respect you more for assisting them when they are harried and will work harder for you.

-**Don't be afraid to uphold store policies.** You can't be fired for doing your job. If this happens because you adhered to a corporate policy, you will win a claim to retain your job.

-**Talk respectfully to staff.** This is a new world and both male and female supervisors cannot get away with "disrespecting" people in the name of a supervisory relationship. There are cases where managers talk to customers with a completely different tone of voice and attitude than they use on their employees. This is unacceptable.

-**Defend your employees.** If you must placate a customer even though they are wrong, do not do it at the expense of your employee. Make sure the customer knows an exception has been made and that the employee was correct in initially questioning them. If circumstances don't allow you to tell the customer this for fear of making matters worse, at least tell the employee they did the right thing. Retail employees suffer from a lack of self-esteem as a result of disrespectful behavior from customers and corporate. It is up to managers to make sure within their store there is a respect for everyone.

-Make sure the store is signed properly. A substantial amount of money is lost when signs are placed on the wrong fixtures or are not changed after sales. Customers seem to have special radar to detect merchandise improperly signed and a substantial amount of money is lost every day. The following is an example of poor signing:

MS. $2.99 (AND UP): This customer came to the register with a Lazy Susan. The price was clearly marked as $9.99, but the customer insisted she should get the item for $2.99 as it was on a shelf with a sign that said $2.99. As it turned out, the department associate missed putting the words AND UP after the $2.99. The customer got the item for $2.99. It was a race between the manager and the other customers on line to see who could get to the area first. The manager was unable to find the AND UP letters and smartly opted for a $9.99 sign to replace the $2.99 sign, thus avoiding the sale of the rest of the $9.99 items for $2.99

-Train employees properly before putting them on the floor. Shoplifters and scammers have a sixth sense about new cashiers. CSR's and other employees and are right there to take advantage. Some common scams which are overlooked by inexperienced employees are merchandise stuffed in suitcases and pocketbooks, returns which do not belong to the store or are improperly tagged, separates deliberately attached together to hopefully be purchased as one piece, ties and other merchandise stuffed in sports coat pockets, forged bills and incorrect change back transactions.

-Don't underestimate the extensive loss of revenue from returns. One scam that is particularly lucrative unfortunately involves unethical cashiers who double bag purchases. The customer buys two of each item but is only charged for one of each item by the cashier. The customer then returns the free items to a different store with the receipt for a full refund. The return amount, which is always cash so that there is no way of identifying the scammer, usually is hundreds of dollars. It can be months or years, or possibly never, before the company catches the cashier in the act of double bagging. Meanwhile, the scammer has hundreds of dollars of free merchandise at home and cash in their pocket as well.

Return fraud is a serious issue and cost retailers billions of dollars a year, losses that are passed on to the consumers. Most people don't believe that they are participating in fraud if they return a used item for full price. They don't think it's wrong to buy an item to use for a special occasion and then return it. These tactics are so pervasive that companies are frantically establishing computer database programs to stop fraudulent or extensive returns.

In closing this section, a strong CSR team is essential but no matter how good they are until store managers and retail owners get some backbone and start adhering to the policies, the return situation will continue to constitute a significant revenue loss for retailers. Customer service is without a doubt the most mentally challenging area of retail to work.

THE PSYCHO SHOPPERS

Why would any woman want to take her husband shopping? Is it some form of spousal abuse or punishment? These men are so miserable and bored waiting outside the fitting room for hours they start flirting innocently with the associates, making small talk to pass the time away. Sometimes they are caught by their wives and get the cold shoulder big time.

On one occasion, two men bonded outside the fitting room after a half-hour waiting for their significant others to finish trying on clothes. One of the shoppers came out and asked her man for his opinion of her outfit. He shrugged and said nothing; which is a typical male reaction when they are put in that position. When the woman disappeared into the fitting room, he told his new male friend how much he hated it when she asked him how she looked. His buddy sympathized with him saying that he often gets in trouble even when he tells his woman she looks good.

And what is it with Mother's Day? It seems as if desperate men encourage their women to spend the entire day in the fitting room of a favorite store as a gift from them while she shops till we drop. It's a family affair as the husbands clear merchandise from

51

tables so they can park their butts on it for a couple of hours and the children provide nourishment and fetch the clothes from the piled-high shopping carts for their mothers.

Most woman try on about 20 outfits for every one purchased. This plays havoc with the fitting room especially on busy weekends. Just two or three woman can literally trash a fitting room leaving clothing strewn everywhere, empty hangers on the floor, price tags removed from clothing, soda and coffee cups and candy wrappers littering the floor, and bodily secretions and food smeared on the mirrors, seats and walls.

On one of our very worst days in the fitting room, we had the farter, the pisser and the crapper. They must have had a meeting the night before to plan that coup.

What is it that makes a customer frantically shop from a return cart or a Z-bar of clothes? Do they think the employees are trying to hide something from them? In most cases, the same items are already on the floor.

Retail employees make crucial decisions every day with regard to what issues to pursue versus what issues to ignore. These decisions are based on who is afraid of who on any given day . . . . the retail cycle is viscous.

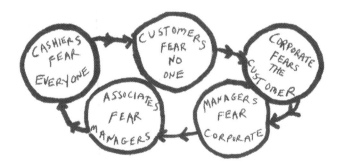

The owners of retail establishments put a lot of emphasis on customer surveys without taking into account the ulterior motives behind them. For instance, if a customer knows they are going to get a discount coupon for complaining and nothing for a compliment, it is a sure bet they are only going to complain. Store employees can please 100 people in a day and make one shopper unhappy and draw a lousy customer service score because of that one complaint. Retailers should give the store managers complete authority regarding customer issues as this duty is an integral part of managing the store and they are in a better place to assess the situation. Executives at home offices continuously reward the deviant behavior of customers thus magnifying the already superior attitude shown toward retail workers and making it more difficult for them to do their jobs.

How many times have employees heard a customer say, "I will never shop here again"? Not only do they come back, but many of them are back in the store within a few minutes of stomping out. If the prices are right, nothing is going to keep them away

Miscommunication is rampant in retail. For example, in one case employees were told repeatedly by managers they could ask to see a customer's receipt if necessary. Based on this directive, an associate asked for a receipt from a customer she saw stealing curtains. The customer immediately went into a tirade loudly proclaiming she did have a receipt for the merchandise. She then brazenly went to the CSR desk and returned the merchandise she had just stolen, without presenting a receipt.

With her significant store credit in hand, the thief then went to the manager's office to complain about the associate who approached her for a receipt. Security is finally watching her on camera but unfortunately didn't get her stealing on film. The manager placates the shoplifter with a discount and then proceeds to admonish the associate for asking her for a receipt, ranting that only security can do this. Security quickly tells him he is wrong and that they can't ask customers to show a receipt until they see them shoplifting on camera. By this time, the associate is livid and informs the manager she will never again ask a customer for a receipt or assist in any way with the prevention of shoplifting.

On her evaluation, the same associate received a glowing rating of exceeding expectations in all job duties with the exception of a comment indicating that "the employee is too aggressive in protecting the company's assets". This was a reference to the receipt incident and is a perfect example of the frustrations involved in working in the retail environment.

For people who work in retail, it is damned if you do, damned if you don't. If an employee is aggressive with customers who are stealing, they are told to back off. If a person walks out with stolen merchandise, the managers rant and rave as to why it happened. If employees refuse to take back items that are not returned in accordance with policies, the customer is irate; if they take back crap that they shouldn't have in order to avoid being abused by the customer, the managers get upset.

There are some serious and interesting psychological issues going on with regard to shopping. The following are examples:

CONDOMS AND THONGS involves an associate finding a used condom in a pair of thong underwear while recovering the lingerie department. It isn't the first condom found in the store; they show up frequently in the fitting rooms, bathrooms, in the ladies' department and among the towels. They are also found in the children's department, which conjures up some really sick images.

MS. PATRIOTIC is very proud of her country, but unfortunately cannot say the same for her integrity. On July 5th, she returns a red, white and blue blouse which she purchased on July 3rd. She complains the blouse has a tear in it and she didn't notice it until she got home. The hole was in the same spot where she pinned her American flag or other patriotic brooch to celebrate July 4th. However, she is a cut above those customers who return their patriotic tees on July 5th worn and with no explanation other than that the item has obviously served its purpose.

MR. AND MS. BROKEN ZIPPER are the people who see something totally different when they look in the mirror. They buy items that are three sizes too small for them and then bring them back with broken zippers and busted seams. That is, if they haven't already destroyed the item in the fitting room and abandoned it for the associates to damage out. This should be a cardinal rule: if you need help to zipper up a dress or pair of pants, it's a sure bet the item doesn't fit you.

MR. AND MS. EL DESTRUCTO are the customers who thrive on trashing the store. Within the time span of 15 minutes, one customer deliberately overturned a basket filled with jewelry, proceeded to fill the now empty basket with other merchandise she had collected, spilled a bottle of glitter glue all over a pile of back-to-school folders, dropped a large glass candle holder, shattering it into a hundred pieces; and opened up ten bags of curtains, leaving them strewn all over the department.

MR. AND MRS. TRASH IT completely destroyed the home fashions department in less than five minutes. The secret fantasy of the employees working in house wares is to follow a customer home, take their curtains down and throw them on the floor, walk all over them, spill drinks on their rugs, and blow their noses in their towels.

MS. AND MR. FILL IT UP AND WALK AWAY are the shopaholics who load up carts until they can't get another thing in them and then abandon them somewhere in the store. Even worse, are the patients (customers), who buy everything in their carts and return all of it within hours because of "shopper's remorse". Everyone in retail owes a special "thanks" to a famous television psychiatrist who recommended his clients with shopping issues fill up and abandon their carts to cope with the problem. Hope he keeps any more advice about shopping to himself.

WHO IS THE BITCH involves a cashier helping a very old lady get her cart out of the store because she could barely see over the top of it. While exiting the store, the door accidentally closed in the face of another customer, who immediately called the little old lady a bitch. The cashier apologized but made a comment to the irate customer that the old lady did not deliberately close the door on her. All of a sudden, the male companion of the woman who insulted the octogenarian got in her face and told her she was the bitch, not the old lady. Sparks were flying between the couple as they walked to their car. Meanwhile, the old lady shouted very politely after them "you two could benefit from an anger management session".

WITH A FRIEND LIKE THIS, WHO NEEDS ENEMIES is about a customer who returned nine boxes of candy she purchased three months prior, complaining they were stale. She paid $1.00 for each box as they were 70% off at the time of original purchase. They were probably very close to their expiration date by the time she purchased them. She was very upset with everyone in the store, announcing she planned to give the candy as gifts to friends that weekend. Not only is she not a very good friend, but she is also at the top of our list for a cheapskate award.

TOO MUCH ON HIS PLATE is the customer who doesn't know where one store begins and another one ends. One of the cashiers frantically called the CSR and said a shopping cart filled with merchandise was out of the store and in the mall. An employee retrieved the cart and as she was pushing it back in the store, a man approached her shouting it was his cart. She explained to him he was not supposed to bring the merchandise out of the store to which he replied that "he thought the mall was all one big store". He said that he needed to get his lottery numbers before the deadline and gave the cashier $100 to hold his merchandise until he finished. True to his word, about five minutes later he came back to the register and purchased his items.

WAIVING THE WHITE FLAG is about customers who leave their underwear behind (not on their behind, but in the store). One of our managers was cleaning the shelves in menswear when she unearthed a dirty pair of men's briefs. She wrestled them onto a hanger and went marching through the store towards damages calling out the names of co-workers so that she could show them her find. Used underwear is left behind frequently in all the fitting room.

ANYTHING FOR A DISCOUNT describes the customer who stabs herself with a loose security tag to get a percentage off her purchase. Granted, you can hardly see the puncture, but the "hurting yourself" scam works every time . . . and she knows it.

MS. OFFICE PURSE involves the customers whose purses look like file cabinets. It takes them forever to find the receipts for their returns. Of course, they don't begin looking for coupons, credit cards, cash or checks until they get up to the cash register, no matter how much time they have had to prepare.

FULL MOON SUNDAYS describes the worst day of the week for customer behavior. It is ironic, but of all the days you would expect people to display good conduct it would be on Sunday . . . . not so! One Sunday, the store was only open for two hours and already there were four shoplifters, a family hiding merchandise in their baby carriage, a young boy stealing computer games, and a man trying to steal a suit who had enough nerve to cover it himself with a plastic bag from a register.

Other Sunday mishaps include customers misplacing their carts and going nuts, screaming and yelling through the store about a conspiracy. Eventually, most carts are found close to where they were last seen. Some customers have the nerve to leave their carts unattended for hours and then pitch a fit when the merchandise cannot be found.

Some of our most serious money issues occur on Sundays. The cashiers are constantly challenged by customers who insist they gave them more money than they did, requiring the registers to be shut down and the contents counted. On very rare occasions are the customers right. Makes one wonder how beneficial the Sunday sermons are, especially with regard to stealing.

Just some of the additional Sunday issues included a customer who had a heart attack, a young man walking around the mall with one of the store's bathing suits on his head, the electricity going out for almost a half-hour with no propane in the generator, and a customer pulling down his pant's zipper in front of two young employees.

FULL MOON WEEK involves an entire week of full moons. A young man came into the store the first day and proceeded to destroy televisions and other electronic equipment for no apparent reason. The next day people were passing counterfeit American Express checks. The next day carts full of merchandise were being dumped all over the store. For the entire week, shoplifting was at an all time high and customers and store associates were losing their tempers at the slightest provocation.

Also, during this week an employee found a child wandering in the lingerie department. He was hysterical and the associate panicked herself when she saw he had no clothes on from the waste down. He was about four years old. Despite the pessimistic first impression he might have been assaulted, it turned out he had gone to the bathroom and was looking for help. He smelled very bad and was shaking as the staff attempted to console him with words only making sure not to touch him in any way.

Where was his mother during all this? Good question as she didn't show up for at least five minutes after frantic announcements were made on the intercom. She was eerily calm and unconcerned over the plight of her child and gave him a stern look when she saw him. There were no hugs or words of comfort from this cold you-know-what. She marched him out the door on a rainy and dank day making no attempt to cover him up. It was a sad situation for everyone and there are clearly no comics to draw to lighten up this situation.

MS. AND MR. I DON'T WANT TO GO HOME are the customers who don't have a life and are the last to leave the store when it closes. Their faces are also pressed up against the door before the store opens in the morning.

THE WIFE BEATER describes a good looking customer who comes into the store and returns two dress shirts complaining the fabric is so thin he can see his undershirt through the material. He touches the dress shirt he has on remarking proudly on the quality of the material in the shirt. The CSR can't resist telling him she can see he has on a "wife beater" undershirt. He turns beet red. For those of you who don't know what that is it's the sleeveless undershirts men who are arrested for assaulting their wives or girlfriends are usually wearing.

MY TIME IS PRECIOUS explains the customers who butt into all transactions complaining that they are in a hurry and need to be waited on right away. They shoot daggers at the cashiers and other customers when they are told they need to wait their turn. In many cases, after they finally complete their transaction they are observed leisurely shopping in another part of the store.

JUST TRY IT describes the customers who have a completely unrealistic idea of their financial status. While applying for a credit card, they present the CSR with a non-major credit card insisting she "just try it". When it doesn't work, they then give the rep a telephone card insisting again she "just try it". When it fails also, they finally present a Master Card that expired three years ago. You guessed it; they insist she "just try it". Eventually, after a painful amount of time, they finally shrug and give up, some quietly and some spouting lots of unprintable words as they walk away. Meanwhile, the associate prays that they won't find another card in their wallet or purse.

I DON'T UNDERSTAND explains the customers who use their language as a way to make negative comments or confuse the employees. One group of customers was overheard talking in Spanish about a friend of theirs who worked as a cook in a restaurant and who never washed his hands. They were red-faced when our bilingual cashier remarked that she would never eat at that restaurant again. Associates observe customers speaking English as they shop the store but when they get to the registers all of a sudden they don't understand it.

MS. LINT LADY is just one of the many needy customers constantly coming to guest services for one thing or another. This particular customer demanded a lint remover and when the CSR couldn't find one, insisted she give her a roll of tape so she could remove lint from her clothes she claimed she picked up walking through the rug department. The CSR was grateful that at least she didn't do what other customers have done; namely, steal a lint lifter, use it and dump it somewhere in the store.

Tape measures, paper, pens, pencils, scissors, money and use of a phone are other things requested, and sometimes demanded, by shoppers.

MY FEET ARE SPECIAL describes the customer who took off her sandals and proceeded to rub her bare, dirty feet over three massage pillows she had thrown on the floor. The dumbfounded CSR who was observing the scene asked her if she wanted to pay for the pillows at the CSR desk or if she could get her a pair of socks to put on her feet if she was going to continue to rub them all over the pillows. The customer had the audacity to give the CSR the finger as she walked away in a huff, leaving the pillows on the floor.

THE MERCHANDISE AND THE ORANGE is about customers who return items without making any effort to clean them. For example, a juicer was brought back with the remnants of an orange still in it. In another instance, a vacuum was returned by an irate customer who was upset that it had broken down. When it was opened, it was filled with wet kitty litter.

MS. IT'S NEVER ENOUGH describes customers who return items because they don't think they were given the right discount even though they have practically gotten everything for free.

MR. EL DESTRUCTO returned a jacket within 20 minutes of purchasing it with no tags attached and a rip in the pocket. Of course, he had already lost the receipt.

MS. SWINGER came to guest services empty-handed except for a handful of screws which she threw on the desk demanding a full refund for a swing she recently purchased. She complained loudly she didn't get all the hardware with the item and became livid when she was informed she would have to bring back the entire swing in order to get a refund. The screws she left behind when she stormed off were saved for months, but she never came back.

MR. NO JACKET swaggered in with the pants to a suit and slapped them down on the counter demanding to exchange them for a bigger size. It took a long time to explain to him the jacket and pants he bought were a suit and they could not be sold or returned separately.

THE BLACK-EYED SCAMMER tried to return several items that were not ours. She was so belligerent everyone figured she got the black eye she was sporting at another store trying to return stuff. Unfortunately, the black-eye worked for her as the manager on duty was sympathetic and agreed to take back her crap, warning her that this would be the last time he would make an exception. That is, unless she came back to the store with another black eye.

MS. SWITCHED TICKET returns maternity clothes the store doesn't carry with children's clothing tags on them. She thinks it's perfectly fine to do that; after all, the two departments do have something in common.

MS. GRIEF STRICKEN brings back receipts and shoes she found in the back of her mother's closet after her death. These items are over seven-years old. After a half-hour of haggling with the shoe manager, she walked away with a couple of bucks in her pocket. She would have been better off giving the shoes to charity and writing them off.

MS. THEY JUST DON'T FEEL RIGHT dropped a pile of towels on the returns counter complaining they just didn't feel right all the while running her fingers over them repeatedly. The CSR had to literally wrestle the towels away from her. Three days later, she came back with more towels lamenting they didn't feel right either. Again, she wouldn't stop touching them and the CSR had to pry her fingers away from the towels. However, this time she had removed the price tags and the manufacturer's tags from the towels. She was asked why she cut out the tags and replied they didn't feel right. The CSR suspected that the tags were cut out so that the returns person wouldn't know they had been washed. The CSR returned the towels but informed the customer this would be the last time that towels she bought would be returned without tags . . . . no matter how they felt.

BRING BACK ANYTHING AND EVERYTHING describes the young couple who were astonished when the CSR refused to return one of their wedding gifts because the store didn't stock it and never had. As they were leaving, the bride was overheard complaining to her groom that her mother was wrong when she told her that the store took back anything and everything.

It is astounding how customers can sniff out a new customer service employee. They immediately begin to return all of their crap and play out all the different return scams until the CSR is more experienced.

It's time to acknowledge some very special customers.

Those who tape the bottom of the shoes they purchase so they will look like they haven't been worn when they return them a couple of months later.

Those who complain about the way the cashier puts change in their hands.

Those who bring in well-worn shoes they have used for three months, complaining that they are uncomfortable.

Those who sew the store's designer labels into cheaper merchandise from other stores and then return the altered clothing. Sadly, most times they get away with it. However, this scam is disappearing because most people don't know how to sew anymore.

Those who come to the register with a coupon issued to the first 300 shoppers and ask, as they wave the coupon, how the cashier will know they were one of the first 300 customers. (Hint: You wouldn't have the coupon if you weren't one of the first 300 customers.)

Those who return merchandise purchased years ago and become outraged when they discover the items aren't worth anything.

The customer who returned a bottle of water she already started drinking even before she paid for it, complaining that the "ozone" in it tasted very bad.

Those who let their children stand up in shopping carts.

Those who let their children take charge of the shopping carts, slamming them into clothing racks and worse yet into other customers.

Those who misplace their cell phones and then leave their cell phone number at customer service as a contact.

Those who return clothing they have bought for a special function they swear they didn't attend, but forget to take the program out of the pockets.

Those who return suits they insist they never wore with a tie in one of the pockets.

Those who demand a receipt for an item they returned, even though they didn't have a receipt for the item to begin with.

Those who return pocketbooks they say they didn't use loaded with makeup, breath mints and other assorted items.

Those who would look much better in the items they are returning rather than the ones they are wearing.

Those who return a phone proclaiming everything worked great with it except they couldn't make or receive calls.

Those who get so caught up in great sales they go crazy. One customer bought seven bottles of nail polish she thought was eye shadow. Imagine her surprise when she put that bright blue nail polish on her eyelids. Of course, she returned them even though they were only a nickel a piece.

Those who return merchandise with no tags on them and then go ballistic when the CSR calls a department specialist to verify the items.

Those who walk on the mops and brooms as the associates are cleaning up urine, crap, broken glass, ice cream, coffee, coke and other assorted spills.

Those who ignore warning signs used to cordon off sections of the store because of a possible risk. Even if the ceiling is falling down, they will risk life and limb to snag a purchase. Or could they be paving the way for a lawsuit?

Those who take all the price tags off of their purchases before they decide whether to keep them.

Those customers who go nuts because the CSR messes up their receipt by crossing out the return items even when they are not getting the receipt back. If they were getting the receipt back, it is still imperative that the CSR cross out the items they are returning so they can't return them again as in the case of double bagging or shoplifting.

The self-absorbed customer who plops a used toilet seat down on the counter to return and then gets insulted when the associate runs for rubber gloves and a bag to contain it.

Those self-centered customers who call the store on a busy weekend and ask the person who answers the phone to find an item in the clearance section, giving a vague description of it. Most of the time, there are thousands of items in clearance and it is like looking for a needle in a haystack to find something specific. Usually, when the item cannot be found even after a good faith effort to look for it, the customers are clearly annoyed.

The customer who returns deodorant swearing it was never used, but when opened has hair all over it. Somebody's dog must smell pretty good.

Those who answer their cell phones or continue phone conversations during checkout or returns making it impossible for the employee to communicate with them about their order. They then question the transaction after they finish their call.

The customer who returned a pair of jeans that smelled like urine, leaving an appointment card with a date to see a urologist in one of the pockets . . . . hopefully, he got some help.

The customers who buy new appliances and return their broken appliances in the new box.

The customer who buys an expensive dress and a cheap dress and puts the expensive tag on the cheap dress to return. If the designer name, size and color on the tag match the dress, the customer always gets away with this scam.

Retailers have to take a lot of the blame for allowing customers to get away with blatant returns in the interest of maintaining good customer relations. *Unfortunately, the customers above are not going to make any store successful, and it is not a good business practice to enable them to continue to steal.*

All retail employees are mentally and physically abused. They have been spit on and hit by irate customers, have had merchandise thrown at them, have been called every name in the book, and have received all the glares and stares known to man.

The customers always provide some form of entertainment. Unfortunately, on most days the serious issues far outnumber the comical events.

One day, an elderly man was asked to leave the store for trying on ladies underwear in the fitting room.

On another occasion, the manager escorted an elderly man out of the store because he was taking pictures of one of the young female employees without her consent. He told the manager he only did it because his wife didn't do anything for him any more.

A very tense moment ensued one day when a customer accused an associate of being a racist because she wouldn't sell her a mis-mated suit. The store's mis-mate policy is that no mis-mates are sold under any circumstances and so does not exclude anyone.

On a lighter note, that same day, a precocious 6-year old future model suddenly appeared out of the lingerie department wearing a 44 DDD bright pink bra and proceeded to give the associates a fashion show of different colored bras . . . . everyone was having a blast until her mother caught her.

There are the attempted pick-ups by the customers.

One elderly associate was asked out by a first year college student. She was so shocked and surprised her reaction was an astounding "are you kidding me, I could be your grandmother".

One day, an associate was approached by a mechanical engineer who coincidentally worked for the same company her husband retired from . . . as a mechanical engineer. When he asked her out she politely replied that "she already had someone just like him at home".

THE EMPLOYEES AREN'T ALWAYS RIGHT EITHER

Unfortunately, in the retail environment, the customers aren't the only ones with psychological issues. Even if a person is perfectly sane when they start working in retail, they will eventually end up with problems.

Retail employees perform a multitude of good deeds on a daily basis that go unrecognized.

For example, a customer called at closing time in tears because she left a scarf that she had picked out for her daughter's birthday party that evening on hold, but was sure she was not going to make it to the store before the doors were locked. The CSR assured her that if she was at the store before the registers closed, she would let her in to buy the scarf. Later, the employee got a big hug from the customer for saving the day.

The sad fact is the longer people works in retail and the more they are abused by the customers, the less likely they are to do favors such as the above.

Retail is not easy. It is physically and emotionally demanding and the work is endless. It is all about surviving the day. An employee must be prepared to be a policeman, a warden, a fashion coordinator, a babysitter, a banker, a physician, a cleaning person, and a psychologist. Many people who have been in the business for a long time are retail-weary, losing their tempers very easily at the customers and their fellow co-workers. If the customer isn't always right, neither are the employees. There are some who are justifiably so burned out they should really try to find other types of employment, something that keeps them away from people buying things.

Most of the retail-weary managers ignore as much as possible to keep the peace and keep the help. Just like in every other business, managers are reluctant to come down on slackers unless their behavior is so preposterous as to merit firing. Instead, they look to the worker bees to cover for employees who are not living up to their potential. This is just one of the reasons for the massive turnover rates in the retail business. Interestingly, newer managers and associates try to remind everyone to be kind to each other and to work together as a team until they themselves become jaded.

The majority of workers in retail are young people so managers are babysitters, teachers, mothers and grandmothers, and on really bad days wardens. Nowadays, just keeping stomachs, backs and butts covered is a major chore. One day, a customer slapped her husband because he took a long, leering look at a cashier's partially exposed butt. He defended himself by insisting it wasn't his fault because it was right there in front of him to look at. He was absolutely right. The next day management posted a notice about proper dress and an associate brought in two ugly sweaters for the cashiers to wear at the register if they came in improperly dressed in the future.

One new cashier showed up at the register wearing a black hooded sweatshirt pulled up over his head and a tissues hanging out of each of his nostrils (he claimed he had a cold and couldn't keep his nose from running). He looked like a cross between a bank robber and a rhino. The customers were afraid to get in his line; they didn't know if he was a cashier or if he was robbing the store. Not surprisingly, he didn't last very long.

Keeping the associates away from their cell phones is quite frankly a full time job. They are incredulous when informed they can't make or receive calls while they are working.

One thing is very clear and that is people in retail do not get the respect they deserve. It is a difficult job on the best of days and the constant attention to shoppers day after day can take its toll on even the most even-tempered personality. This results in employees who rarely smile or make eye contact with the customers. The employees have lost the concept of taking pride in a job well down and seem to focus only on getting out of the store, whether it is at the end of their shift or when they retire or die.

Retail employees have low self-esteem and for good reason. Considering what they do, their salaries are ridiculously low. The perception by the public of people who work in retail being uneducated and unable to get so-called "better" jobs is totally unjust and without merit.

It takes a lot of knowledge, effort, patience, integrity and common sense to run a successful store by keeping the goods flowing, the customers happy, corporate satisfied, the store adequately staffed, and making a profit in addition to all that. Every person in the chain has to do their part under strained circumstances each and every day. The retail employee is constantly on the firing line never knowing when the fur will fly or when he/she will experience a full moon Sunday, when everything goes wrong from computer/register/phone malfunctions to breakages to employee no-shows, to customer issues, to not meeting quota because of slow sales and shrinkage (theft from both customers and employees).

Some advice to retailers interested in increasing employee self-esteem, productivity and retention:

Don't give the store away to the customers while refusing to pay employees a decent salary. This practice is one of the most upsetting to retail workers.

Don't take away valuable benefits from employees.

Defend employees against customer complaints that are not valid. Allow managers to settle disputes within the store at the time of the incident.

Stop installing rigid time clocks which penalize employees if they are a few minutes late for work but fail to acknowledge employees who work during breaks and lunches because of staff shortages.

Boost employee morale with positive survey data rather than constant negative comments. After finishing a demanding shift, it is demoralizing to listen to how many customer complaints were lodged.

On most days, retail stores are seriously understaffed due to no shows and call offs. The turnover rate is also very high. Stores lose hundreds of employees a year. Some new hires work for only one day or do not show up at all. There are a lot of issues causing this phenomenon.

Many young people don't want to or don't have to work because they are being supported by their parents. When they do accept a job, they tend to bail out quickly because of the low salary and stressful work environment which they have a hard time coping with.

Access to money and unlimited merchandise is too much temptation for not only the customers but employees, many of whom are fired because of theft.

Employee no-shows are the most serious issue that managers face. Many workers bury at least four parents and as many grandparents in less than a year. In this day and age, this is highly likely with all the extended family situations; however, in most cases these bogus deaths are just excuses to get out of work. The employees sometimes get confused themselves and report the same relative's death twice. Many of the supposedly deceased people eventually end up shopping in the store.

For example, an employee didn't show up for work for a week reporting that "her mother had a heart attack". Months later, her mother was shopping in the store and a concerned associate asked her how she was feeling after her heart attack. Later, many staff members observed the mother at her daughter's register giving her a stern lecture about telling such a horrendous lie.

Other excuses associates use for not showing up for work include not being able to find a babysitter even though they don't have a child, broken down cars even though they don't have a car or for that matter a license, stolen cars even though they drive it to work the next day without any explanation as to how it suddenly was found, and no clothes to wear as everything they own is dirty.

There are plenty of places for non-productive employees to hide out. An employee was locked in a store overnight because he fell asleep in the second floor storage area and didn't hear the closing announcement.

The home fashions department is a popular place for the employees to congregate. They fold and refold towels while they socialize. On second thought, maybe that's why a customer thought the towels just didn't feel right!

On the other hand, the employees avoid curtains like the plague. They will ignore for days drapes separated from their bags and leave regular priced curtains mixed in with promotional curtains and vice versa. Corporate will not allow signs to be posted requesting customers to refrain from opening bags of merchandise, even though display curtains are hung so the customer can see what the curtain looks like. Ironically, after the bag is opened and the curtain is dropped on the floor, the customer will reach for an unopened bag to buy. This holds true for underwear, socks and all other bagged items.

On one occasion, a wicker basket made its way to the register and when the cashier opened it, it contained a dirty diaper, several pieces of merchandise and a half-eaten bag of candy. In the real world, associates should be policing their assigned areas more frequently during the day to prevent customers from trashing the store or shoplifting. Unfortunately, because of staff shortages they are often stuck on a register for long periods of time while their departments are trashed.

So here's special recognition to those employees whose behavior makes it more difficult for retail employees to get the respect they deserve:

. . . . who give friends empty bags so they can shoplift,

. . . . who don't verify the price of merchandise brought to the register or returned without price tags or receipts,

. . . . who let customers take items out of the store which have not been purchased,

. . . . who fill bags with merchandise and hide them for eventual removal from the store,

. . . . who don't look in pocketbooks, comforters, suitcases and under the carts for hidden items,

. . . . who does not call for approval when a check is declined at the register and instead accepts the rejected check. When the check bounces and the number that was given cannot be confirmed by the check approval company, the store must absorb the loss and the cashier is written up for a register shortage,

. . . . who tells management they have a family emergency and need to leave immediately, and then are caught hanging around outside the store with friends,

The customers aren't the only ones who participate in scams. The following are some examples of associate scams.

The cashier allows a friend to buy two duplicate items but only charges them for one. The friend then brings back one of the items with the receipt for a full refund. The duplicate item they have at home is now free. The ruse is called double-bagging.

The CSR associates ring up bogus return transactions and pocket the cash refunds. Eventually they will be caught, but not before they have stolen a substantial amount of cash.

The associate buys items with their employee discount and then has someone return them without a receipt to get a full refund.

The cashier allows a friend to buy substantial merchandise without paying for it. They cancel the transaction before totaling it but bag the merchandise for their buddy as if it were purchased. Another similar scam is to total the order and ask management for a post void once the partner in crime has left with the stolen merchandise. This scam only worked a few times before management required the customer and merchandise to be present before a void could be done. When security personnel are actually in the store with cameras focused on the registers, they frequently catch cashiers giving friends free merchandise.

Of course, there are the associates who begin stealing cash from the registers immediately hoping to pocket a substantial amount before they are let go. The more desperate the store is for workers, the more likely it is the associate can get away with stealing for a long period of time.

The associates pocket promotional coupons meant for customers and gives them to friends to redeem. During every promotional event, scammers received thousands of dollars in merchandise using the stolen coupons.

Associates outright steal merchandise, putting items in their bags when security is not on duty.

Associates hide regular priced items until they go on deep-discount and then purchase them, scamming the store out of a full price purchase.

SECURITY TO SHOES

So what about security? Ha, ha, ha!!

Each time a customer, manager or another associate is giving an employee a bunch of crap, the comeback line is *"security to shoes"*. This is because some corporate executive actually thinks that announcing this over the intercom every half-hour is going to discourage shoplifters in shoes . . . like the thieves don't know it's a recording.

When employees inform management their friends brag about how easy it is to shoplift from the store, it is a sure thing the security system is not working. *People have to be very confident to actually brag about shoplifting in a place where people they know work.* On the other hand, there are so many stipulations which must be met in order to successfully prosecute thieves, it is almost impossible to catch them.

Security is bare bones. The only thing a "willing" employee can do is try to intimidate potential shoplifters to the extent they give up trying to steal. Keep in mind this process has to be done in a way that will convince the customers they are still valued. *After getting burned a few times, most employees quickly realize it is best not to get involved with security issues at all.*

Allowing packages to come in and out of the store unchecked is a recipe for theft. Retail executives believe this process is insulting to customers. *Interestingly enough, other stores check packages and they have more business . . . . which would lead one to believe people enjoy being insulted.* Hiring people as door greeters is a good business procedure in this day and age, as these people pay for their meager salaries by saving thousands of dollars in theft.

When there are two entrances and exits on opposite sides of the store, people are brazen enough to fill up a cart with items and walk out the opposite exit, claiming that they paid for their items on the "other side" . . . *that is, if they are even approached, which doesn't happen very often.*

People are so confident they will not be caught they actually steal merchandise and immediately bring it to customer service for a return without a receipt . . . . *no questions asked.*

THE $2.99 BUST involved a new employee who observed a young boy about 10 years old putting a toy car in the left pocket of his oversized pants. She followed him to the cash registers and watched as he slipped a candy bar into his right pocket. He joined his mother, father and sister at the register and the associate observed as his mother paid for her purchases and then complained to the cashier that she didn't get some kind of a discount.

Meanwhile, the boy joined his father at the exit door and it was at that point the employee decided to confront them. She told the father it appeared his son had two store items in his pockets he had not paid for. The father made the boy empty his pockets and give back the merchandise. He then proceeded to bring his son outside, asking the associate to accompany them. Once outside, he gave the boy a tongue lashing that befit the occasion.

The problem is this very naïve associate risked the accusation turning sour with negative consequences to her if the father had decided not to cooperate. Corporate would definitely have fired her based on the policy that no confrontation should have occurred in this case. *After all, the kid was just a shoplifter in training.*

THE POTATO CHIPS VERSUS THE POLOS. Security busted an employee for eating a 90-cent bag of potato chips before paying for it. Everyone was elated except for the fired employee. Sadly, on the same day a customer stole four polo shirts at $59.99 a piece, but security missed it.

Most likely, the thief returned the polos to another store *without a receipt and with no questions asked.*

THIS IS THE LAST TIME (NOT). Managers who see repeat offenders will threaten them by saying it will be the last time they return an item for them without a receipt. This line has about as much meaning as *security to shoes.* These customers just wait until the smoke clears and a new CSR or manager is on duty to continue their scam.

Unfortunately, until retail institutes a policy that prohibits returns without receipts, the store manager cannot really enforce this policy, and corporate would definitely not back the manager if the customers complained that they were not allowed to return an item without a receipt

CELEBRATE GOOD TIMES (COME ON?). Occasionally, security does actually catch someone and the staff celebrates for months until the next bust. Employees vary in their enthusiasm for participating in security issues. One associate is suspicious of everyone while another would let a customer walk out of the store with a cart filled with unpaid merchandise and maybe mention it in passing to someone a half-hour later.

THE CLOWN incident happened on Halloween night and involved an employee who was changing display curtains. She was wearing a clown costume complete with mask and was standing on a very high ladder. The store was practically empty of customers, but the employee observed from her fantastic viewpoint a customer stuffing exercise clothing into a bag. The thief then made her way down to customer service to return the stolen items for credit.

When the thief came around the corner, she looked up and saw the clown on the ladder and freaked out shouting loudly that the associate scared the hell out of her. But when the clown calmly announced she saw her shoplifting, she turned and made a beeline out of the store, dropping the bag full of stolen merchandise.

I WASN'T HIRED TO BE A STALKER (WAS I?). Sometimes stalking the customers and constantly asking them if they need help does work, but it is nerve-wracking and takes away from time that should be spent doing other duties. One customer was filling up a huge gift bag with store merchandise until she became uncomfortable with all the attention she was getting from several employees, realizing she was being watched. She eventually dropped the parcel in the luggage department. As the bag was retrieved, one of the associates recognized it from the dollar store. Later, security confirmed that even the bag she used to shoplift had been stolen.

THE DUMPSTER CAPER involved an associate who found herself on top of a huge dumpster helping security dig through garbage to rescue two huge gift bags of merchandise. Ironically, the stolen merchandise valued at $2,000 belonged to stores other than the one she worked for. Not one person from these stores bothered to say thank you for the save.

Later, the associate was chastised by management. She was told she would not have been supported by corporate if the caper had gone bad or she had been hurt, and would have been fired.

YOU'RE FIRED! Sadly, a former security employee for over twenty years was fired because she left the store to pursue a shoplifter and was almost run over by the thief. To add insult to injury, the perpetrator then filed an assault charge against the security guard she tired to kill with her car. *Is it any wonder why shoplifting is so popular?*

THE BABY SNEAKER SWITCH involved a security guard alerting the shoe manager that a woman had been observed putting a new pair of sneakers on her child, dumping the old shoes in the new sneaker box and hiding it on a shelf in another department. ***Unbelievably, the security guard did not see the child enter the store with the old shoes on and therefore was missing a key element for prosecution and was not going to be able to apprehend them.*** Something is definitely wrong with the legal system if this is the case.

In a last ditch effort, security advised the cashier to ask the women for a receipt for the shoes on the baby's feet when she came to the register. The associate complied, but the shoplifter was a pro and quickly responded that she had purchased the shoes the day before and did not have the receipt with her. Even though she got out of the store with the new sneakers, she was very nervous and knew security was on to her. Would it discourage her from shoplifting again? Definitely not!

Employees are encouraged to contribute anti-theft posters to corporate and one enthusiastic associate proudly submitted a few assuming they would be well-received.

**THESE SHOES ARE MADE FOR WALKING
AND THAT'S JUST WHAT THEY'LL DO
IF YOU DON'T KEEP AN EYE ON THE CUSTOMERS
AND YOUR FELLOW ASSOCIATES TOO!!**

FIRST COMES LOVE
THEN COMES MARRIAGE
THEN COMES A CUSTOMER
WITH MORE THAN A BABY IN THE CARRIAGE

BEWARE OF GUESTS SO HIP
COME IN FOR A SUITCASE
AND LEAVE PACKED FOR THE TRIP

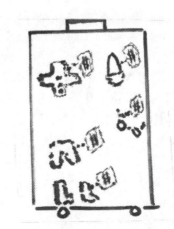

All of the posters were rejected for being too insulting to the customers.

GOOD COP, BAD COP. Part of the mode of operation for shoplifters is to make a scene when they think they are under suspicion. These particular shoplifters call the employees every name in the book and have been known to physically abuse them. They work in pairs or groups and intimidation is their game. Sometimes, they play the good cop/bad cop routine, but almost always they are the bad cops.

THINK QUICK. The customer service representatives are put in precarious positions requiring quick judgments on a daily basis. In one case, a CSR frantically tried to come up with a way to discount regular priced merchandise because she knew shoplifters were heading her way to return clothing they had just stolen. Security was not on duty that day, but another employee had observed the shoplifting. In the end, the quick-thinking CSR gave them only $75 worth of store credit for hundreds of dollars worth of merchandise. ***This was an unusual circumstance as most CSR's will not risk their jobs to antagonize even a shoplifter.***

MAY I SPEAK TO SECURITY? Savvy shoplifters call the store and ask for security. If they are told no one is in or if they are put through to the security office and no one answers, they figure it is a good time to come to the store and shoplift. When security finally caught on and requested that all calls to them require the caller to identify themselves, the shoplifters always hung up.

NO SHOES, BUT A BOXED LUNCH. The shoe department takes a big hit with shoplifters and empty shoe boxes are found in every department. Some brazen people leave their old shoes behind in the boxes, putting them neatly back on the shelves where the new shoes once resided. Actually, it's the only time the boxes are put back where they belong. Some customers leave half-eaten pizzas, sandwiches, chips and candy in shoe boxes. This gives new meaning to the term *boxed lunch.*

NEED NEW EARRINGS, NO PROBLEM. Jewelry is the most popular shoplifted merchandise, costing stores millions of dollars a year. In one day at one store a multitude of empty boxes of jewelry can be found hidden under other merchandise and in the fitting rooms. ***An unattended fitting room is the most popular place to steal jewelry as well as every other item the store sells.***

BONNIE AND BONNIE describes two female customers. Bonnie #1, the driver, waited in the car while her accomplice looked for a good time to exit the store with her cart filled with unpaid merchandise. One of the new cashiers recognized Bonnie #2, who had been apprehended for shoplifting at another store. She informed the CSR who immediately followed Bonnie #2 out to the car and asked for her receipt, grabbing hold of the cart while the customer pretended to search for the receipt. She told the thief the cart would have to come back into the store until she produced a receipt. The customer service representative also bravely, or stupidly depending on who you talk to, reached in the back seat and removed two items that had already made their way out of the shopping cart. While she wheeled the cart inside the store, Bonnie and Bonnie took off in the getaway vehicle. The store had the merchandise back and hopefully the shoplifters were discouraged from coming back again . . . at least for a few weeks.

Of course, Bonnie and Bonnie is another case where the employee was unaware that if the incident had turned out badly, she would not have been supported by corporate. She most likely would have been fired especially if the shoplifters filed a complaint. ***Employees are not supposed to leave the store to pursue a shoplifter under any circumstances, although many of them are not informed about this during their training.***

Security is a very frustrating issue for employees as there are no clear-cut directions for dealing with shoplifters. Most employees eventually make the right decide not to get involved. There are hundreds of other ways to get in trouble in retail without adding to it by being the self-appointed shoplifting guru.

The way businesses are run these days gives customers unlimited options on the way they can rip off an establishment. Some lofty executives believe it is not worth worrying about security because they are getting the merchandise for such low prices that they can afford the loss. The reality is this problem has become so serious that many stores have, are and will be going out of business based strictly on losses from shoplifting. ***Despite the mindset that the company is only losing pennies, this is not the case . . . . it's more like millions and millions of pennies.***

NOT SO SECRET SHOPPERS

This book wouldn't be complete without touching on the subject of secret shoppers. The people hired to check out how employees are performing. Actually, it really doesn't matter how the secret shopper grades the store. What is of paramount importance is how they describe the employee. If an employee is identified in the report as looking ten years younger than they really are, it's a good day even though the employee lost 50 points for the store by not asking or answering the right questions or doing the right thing.

On almost all occasions, the staff knows when the secret shopper is in the store. Even with that knowledge, many of the associates still don't do the right thing. On the other hand, there have been cases where a particular associate was blamed for something when they weren't even working during the time period noted in the report. Not to mention cases where a secret shopper outright lied about an associate's performance. Basically, these reports are not taken very seriously and no one is fired because of them. The staff is bare bones as it is without losing someone to meaningless dribble from someone on the corporate payroll.

CUSTOMER COMMENDATION
(YEAH, JUST ONE)

A gold star goes to the following exemplary customer:

Mr. Honest who returned $150 worth of merchandise the cashier did not charge him for . . . so he could pay for them. He was rewarded with 10% off his entire purchase.

Oh, wait there is another one.

Ms. Security who patiently wore her boots with a security tag on one of them for six months until she could get back to the store to have it removed. Actually, she should probably get another form of recognition too, but that wouldn't be kind.

Well, that's it for customer commendations . . . . REALLY!!

The young ladies below do not deserve a commendation . . . . or maybe they do?

CHEAPSKATE OF THE YEAR AWARDS

MR. $8.88 returned about 35 boxes of 100 count sandwich bags which he had purchased at $.24 a box. He said he found them less expensive somewhere else. The only place he could have gotten them cheaper was out of a trash can.

MR. GENEROUS GRANDPA who was thrilled with himself because he found a toy with two items in it for his grandson. He was ecstatic because he now had both a Christmas and birthday gift for the boy . . . and all for $9.99.

MS.-MATE BATHING SUIT slaps a bathing suit top and bottom on the counter. Each item is individually priced at $2.40 but she demands to get them both for $2.40. The articles are different sizes and have been mis-mated out for that reason. With mis-mates, the customer also gets whatever the lowest markdown is which on this day is 50%. Still not satisfied, she insists she should get both for $2.40 in addition to the 50% off . . . . all this drama to save $1.20. The cashier was thrilled that in this instance the cheapskate did not get her way as the manager on duty had already reached her limit with miserly customers for the day.

MS. CASHMERE switched a ticket on a cashmere sweater which was selling for $16 with 50% off, making it $8. The original price of the sweater was $99. The customer replaced the 50% tag with a 75% clearance tag, making the sweater $4 instead of $8. She was caught, and was completely irate that she had to pay $8, insisting she should not be penalized because "someone else" messed with the ticket . . . . all of this to save $4.

MRS. WIFE OF A CHEAP HUSBAND comes into the store on a regular basis and pays for her purchases with a check.

An hour later, she returns all of the items knowing she will receive cash. This proves there is more than one way to scam a cheap husband.

MR. GASSY who demanded the manager reimburse him money for the gas he used to return his purchases to the store.

MR. DENIED HIS DOG who returned a pair of slippers that had obviously been chewed on by an animal. He insisted they were bought that way and swore he didn't have a dog. The slippers were damaged and the reason given by the CSR was "chewed on by the customer".

CITATIONS FOR "SPECIAL" CUSTOMERS

THE MARATHON MAN award to the customer who came into the store ten minutes before closing and bought $109 worth of merchandise to the register. He even managed to use the bathroom during that short period of time.

THE MOST PERSISTENT award to the customers who insisted the employee in luggage pack a suitcase with 99 pounds of merchandise to make sure that it would indeed hold the advertised weight. And an EMPLOYEE OF THE YEAR award to the good-natured associate who provided the bathroom scale and the merchandise to pack in the suitcase.

THE BIGGEST LAUGH award to the three children who came running to customer service because they heard the announcement over the loudspeaker saying "kids to customer service". The CSR was actually calling the children's department manager for a price check.

THE MOST DESTRUCTIVE award to the five year old with a huge chocolate ice cream cone in her hand, riding a pink tricycle from toys through the ladies department. Before she could be stopped, she left a smear of ice cream on an entire row of dresses.

And, finally, *THE MOST OBNOXIOUS* award to the customers who whistle at employees to get their attention. The only help they will get using that tactic is from a stray dog.

TRASH, TRASH AND MORE TRASH

With all the talk about the greening of America, nothing has been mentioned about the most serious threat to our planet . . . . and it comes from retail. It is mind boggling the magnitude of packing material used to get merchandise from point A to point B. Retailers should be required to recycle. Even if everyone in the United States drove an electric car, it would not compensate for the amount of trash that ends up in dumps from retail stores. Be afraid . . . . be very afraid!

THE TOP TEN LIST

The following are the top ten questions retail employees would like to ask customers:

1. Why do you continue to buy clothing for your children and grandchildren? They always return everything.

2. Why do you bring your children with you when you plan to shoplift or lie about returns? "But Daddy, don't you remember you did wear those shoes to Aunt Karen's wedding?"

3. What do you do with all the clothes you buy? You dress like a homeless person when you come into the store to shop.

4. Why do you wait until five minutes before you have to meet your kids at the bus stop to get into the checkout line?

5. Why do you buy merchandise the size of an elephant and try to fit it into your clown car?

6. Why do you bring your tired and hungry kids shopping and then scream at them or slap them when they get cranky?

7. Why do you get upset when an associate is called to verify your returns when the tags are not attached and you have no receipt?

8. Why do you continue to shop in the store after you have screamed at us "that you will never shop in the store again"? Do you think we can't see you coming back in?

9. Why don't you buy the package of underwear you open? At least you can be sure you are actually getting what you want.

10. Why are you always complaining you can't lose weight, but you never bend down to pick up items you drop on the floor or return items you don't want to their proper place in the store?

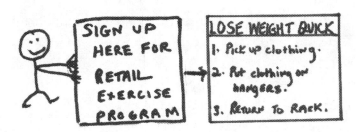

LIQUIDATION

People will only get away with whatever you let them get away with, including destroying your business. Eventually, poor business practices by retailers result in the following:

When this happens, the liquidation process begins. It involves getting rid of all the merchandise in preparation for closing the store. For a person working in retail, it can be a fantastic experience . . . the light at the end of the tunnel so to speak. As each piece of merchandise leaves the store, the time frame for dealing with customers shortens. There is no need to worry about new merchandise. The focus is on condensing the store as merchandise sells down. It's an interesting and rewarding experience.

The store's closing allows retail workers to bend the rules. For instance, a fitting room attendant brazenly challenged a known shoplifter by asking her if she "intended to buy anything after spending over three hours in the fitting room". The customer immediately complained to the liquidator, who confronted the fitting room attendant. She defended herself by saying "it's about time somebody told these customers that they aren't going to be able to steal anything no matter how long they hang around the fitting room". The liquidator put up her hands and walked away.

Sadly, the retailer who owned the business authorized fitting room attendants as a last ditch effort to save the business . . . . but the action was too little, too late, just like the mandate to check bags coming in and out of the store.

Other silliness included the last delivery truck from corporate which was the size of a sperm whale and contained only four boxes. Two of them were stuffed with job applications and the other two boxes contained thousands of foot sox for trying on shoes. Ironically, there were only a few dozen shoes left in the store.

After the store had a closing date, corporate finally allowed the use of the following statement:

DO NOT OPEN BOXES, PACKAGES OR CARTONS

The managers would have benefited from a directive like that years earlier. But at this point it was utterly ridiculous as there were only a dozen packages or boxes of anything left in the store.

Over the years, the store lost millions of dollars in jewelry and fragrance thefts which was to be expected because these items were not secured. Too late, the company made a half-hearted attempt to secure certain items with special locks.

A few months before the bankruptcy, the following directive arrived from the corporate office:

FOR THE CONVENIENCE OF OUR CUSTOMERS DURING THE HOLIDAY SEASON, PLEASE UNLOCK ALL FRAGRANCE AND JEWELRY AREAS

However, during the liquidation process when the most expensive watch was $4.95, they were locked up tighter than Fort Knox. Go figure!

FINAL SALE and **NO RETURNS** means be sure you want the item before you walk out of the store with it.

Part of the liquidation process includes selling the fixtures. As racks were emptied they were broken down and stored in the back of the store. What is it about bright yellow caution tape with big black letters DO NOT ENTER that makes people want to do just that? Why do people allow their supposedly precious children to play in such areas?

Shoplifters were so traumatized when they lost their two favorite shoplifting areas, they brazenly complained about it loud enough for all to hear.

One customer's reaction to the store closing:

The last Sunday the store was open was a full moon Sunday and the following occurred:

One customer was upset when she couldn't return an item. She obviously didn't understand that the store was no more.

Special receipts were issued with each sale with huge black letters saying **ALL SALES FINAL.**

Two entertaining bachelor's approached the jewelry department just days before the store closed. Everything was gone with the exception of some cologne testers for men, which were being sold at a ridiculously low price. The men started a conversation with the cashier about their problems with woman. Later, she overheard them discussing the purchase.

The store always had problems with a leaky roof. It rained heavily a few days before the store closed, and one of the frequent customers was a victim. His response was very good-natured as well as amusing.

The store was closed for a week, but the fixture liquidators were still on site when the following took place:

IN CLOSING (THE BOOK, NOT ANOTHER STORE)

The last security person hired by the company was gay. She was one of the most entertaining people in the store and everyone but the managers thought she was the greatest thing since sliced bread. She spent lots of time in her office looking at the security cameras observing the racks. Unfortunately, she was looking at the wrong racks. She was trying to find a girlfriend. This gives new meaning to the term "shopping the racks".

Despite the security person, people were still stealing even when prices were so low you couldn't get better deals at the dollar store. While the fitting room attendant was at lunch, one shoplifter had the nerve to abscond with an entire wardrobe and leave her old clothes behind, with the price tags from the stolen items in the pocket of her dirty old jeans. This is another example of the importance of a good fitting room attendant and the lack of business sense of companies that don't monitor the fitting rooms.

Retail employees were asked the following question:

"What is your biggest gripe about working in retail?"

"Honestly, it's the money. We literally work our tails off for minimum wage."

"The way we get treated by customers. There is no respect for our profession."

"I get so upset with people who think just because I work in retail, I must be stupid. A teacher asked me to figure out the square footage of his living room so he could buy the right amount of hardwood flooring. He still continued to treat me like a second-class citizen even after I did what he couldn't do with his degree."

"I hate the union. They take money out of my paycheck every week and I get nothing for it."

"Why is it that people can get away with stereotyping all blondes as dumb when it isn't politically correct to do it with anyone else? Perfect strangers approach me to tell me blonde jokes because I am blonde. Well, let me tell you I have NEVER had a blonde person come up to me and ask me what the cost of their purchase would be with 10% off, but I sure have had plenty of brunettes ask me that question. Isn't that simple math you learned in elementary school?"

A male employee listening to the above conversation added the following:

"I've always wondered about this. If a brunette dyes her hair blonde does she immediately become dumb?"

"Please tell clothing designers to put their names in all of their clothing so that when two and three piece garments are separated it is easier to reunite them. So what's the big deal? Spending days mating clothes is no fun."

"Do you know how many children I have seen fall out of shopping carts because their ###### parents let them stand up?

When I warn them they need to make the child sit down, they gave me dirty looks and tell me to mind my own business. Then when the kid falls on its head, they expect me to help and to sympathize with them as if it wasn't their fault."

"I'm having a t-shirt made for myself. It says:

I SURVIVED WORKING IN RETAIL WITHOUT HURTING ANYONE."

"People, please practice time management. Don't shop until you have to be somewhere in five minutes and expect the cashier to make up the time. We are not miracle workers. The reality is as it gets more difficult to hire people to work in retail, the lines will get longer."

"Manufacturers need to sell all bathing suit tops and bottoms separately. There are millions of people in this world who are apple and pear shaped and selling bathing suits as separates would make these fruits very happy."

"You don't want me to answer that. I'm tired of people thinking that just because a person takes good care of themselves they must be shallow. I like to look and dress nice and I don't appreciate people kidding me about it with comments like why are you so dressed up? Sorry, but this subject really gets me hot. Thank you for letting me vent."

"What's up with people who fill shopping carts with clothes and then abandon them in the store? Why don't they just see a therapist to find out why they do this because obviously they need help?"

"So what would happen to me if I stereotyped other people the way they stereotype me for working in retail? I'm sure nothing good, but here goes anyway. This is anonymous, right?

1. People of a certain size are lazy. They consistently leave clothes piled on the floor of the fitting room for people of another size to pick up, fold and hang.

2. There is a particular group of people who are very bad parents. They are always losing their children in the store and when they are found, slap them silly as if it is the child's fault they got lost.

3. Ugly people are mean. Yep, the uglier a person is the meaner they are. Or maybe they just look ugly because they are so mean.

4. There is a certain group of people who have absolutely no class at all, but I wouldn't dream of identifying them. I wouldn't want to hurt anyone's feelings like mine are hurt every time a customer looks down on me for working in retail."

"Why do people act like they are in kindergarten? They only hang up their clothes, pick things up off the floor, or return things to the racks when someone is watching them. Otherwise, they leave the merchandise strewn all over the place."

"If customers think moaning and groaning and complaining loudly in front of the employees about how messy the store is or how long the lines are is doing any good, they can guess again. The expectations of people working in retail are not realistic in view of staff shortages. A cashier or floor associate has no control over any of the issues customers are griping about and, at some point, stop listening to preserve their own sanity."

"My biggest gripe is customers who act like squirrels hiding their nuts for the winter. They put clothes and other items under the seats in the fitting rooms, under the clothing racks, behind shoe boxes, and in any hiding place they can find in the store."

"People who hang up their clothes inside out. I don't know why this bothers me so much because I should be grateful they hang up their clothes at all. I swear most young people don't even know how to use a hanger."

"Can't people treat the bathrooms in stores the way they would their own? On second thought, they probably don't flush the toilet at home, leave toilet paper all over the floor, write profanity on the walls, flush price tags or sanitary napkins down the toilet, and leave dirty infant and adult diapers on the floor."

"Managers should not be afraid to discipline anyone who doesn't do their job. If an employee's lack of work ethic is properly documented, there should be no repercussions for firing such people. I am sick and tired of a lot of my co-workers getting away with not doing their jobs."

"All I can say is retail companies must have loads of money because they certainly don't take security seriously. It is amazing nowadays how easy it is to steal. Security is almost non-existent and everyone is afraid to accuse people of anything for fear of being sued."

"Women can buy all the new clothes they want, but if they abuse other people or trash the store in the process of getting them, there is no way they are ever going to feel good about themselves no matter how nicely they are dressed. Also, to people who steal, watch out for bad karma. It definitely will come your way eventually."

The answers to the above survey won't solve world peace but if customers would try to respect the retail profession, the people working in it and the merchandise they sell, retail employees might be able to overcome their lack of self-esteem and treat customer with genuine courtesy instead of the forced deference mandated by corporate.

Remember, when it comes to retail there will always be **SECURITY TO SHOES (a.k.a. BULLCRAP).**